The British Virgin Islands

The British Virgin Islands

The Hometown Lowdown Guide to Travel and Taste

Paul Spicer

iUniverse, Inc.
New York   Bloomington

The British Virgin Islands
The Hometown Lowdown Guide to Travel and Taste

iUniverse books may be ordered through booksellers or by contacting:

iUniverse
1663 Liberty Drive
Bloomington, IN 47403
www.iuniverse.com
1-800-Authors (1-800-288-4677)

ISBN: 978-0-595-42153-4 (pbk)
ISBN: 978-0-595-86493-5 (ebk)

Printed in the United States of America

iUniverse rev. date: 7/6/2009

"One of the best ways to learn about a culture is to explore their food and local dishes. Paul Spicer provides a valuable insight into the BVI culture within the pages of the British Virgin Islands: The Hometown Lowdown Guide to Travel & Taste–with prized recipes, folklore, and valuable bits of travel information."

—Donna Arter, Chef and Director, Hawks Nest Management Ltd, Tortola, British Virgin Islands

"Never has an island cookbook included so much useful information, from where to find lobster or how to beat your conch. British Virgin Islands: The Hometown Lowdown Guide to Travel & Taste has authentic island recipes along with a good dose of entertaining history and island info. Learn to cook the island way and enjoy a potpourri of exotic flavors and tastes. You will be hard pressed to set this page turner down, once you start reading. British Virgin Islands: The Hometown Lowdown Guide to Travel & Taste is sure to become a treasured book for everyone who has ever set foot on our sandy shores. If you haven't visited the British Virgin Islands, this book will convince you that life ain't worth living until you've been to the BVI and tasted island flavor."

—Dear Miss Mermaid, Weather Correspondent for Tortola, British Virgin Islands (DearMissMermaid.com)

"British Virgin Islands: The Hometown Lowdown Guide to Travel & Taste is a must-have for every islander, visitor and tourist to the beautiful British Virgin Islands. Learn about culture, history, food and best of all the heavenly recipes that will make you want to pirate a ship and sail to the islands, where the mangos are fresh and the bananas sweet and life is thoughtfully slower. Reading The Hometown Lowndown Guide to Travel & Taste will make you think you are in the islands already and you might even catch DIF (Dreaded Island Fever: that feeling that if you don't get back to the islands soon, you'll just die of a broken heart.)"

—Cynthia Rose, Tortola Private Chef Service, Author of "Fine Fare with Flair"

In Memory of Norwell Durant—
A true BVIslander and the greatest sea salt harvester

Acknowledgements

Walter Andes, Doug and Donna Arter, Malcolm Boyes, BVI Tourist Board, Marge Ewert, Hunter Butler, Peter Farley, Kyle and Judy Lynn, Jerry O'Connell, Julian Putney, Anne Reil, Cynthia Rose, Jim Rudy, Melvin and Mildred Spicer, Stuart and Carson Spicer, Hew Stith, Travel Talk Online, Rachele Walter, Zimmerman Agency

Contents

Foreword

When I first went down to the beautiful British Virgin Islands back in 1984, fine cuisine was hardly the reason to discover "Nature's Little Secrets": the spectacular beaches, the cooling trade winds carrying the sounds of talented musicians, and the smiling people were enough to feed anyone's soul.

There certainly was some good food to be found—amazing lobster patties at Jule's Place in Carrot Bay, and the barbeque at The Bomba Shack cooked on an old wheel rim. Every Friday night under the spreading banyan tree in Little Apple Bay there would be the local fish fry, a tradition that still goes on today.

What a difference a few years can make.

These days the BVI's are dotted with the greatest eateries. There are world class restaurants like Brandywine, The Dove, Spaghetti Junction, and for a wonderful meal with a view-to-die-for Bananakeet Café above Carrot Bay is world class. There are spectacular local eateries: Coco Plums and Palm's Delight are terrific local hangouts with fine food. It's hard to beat Lou's famed pirate hideaway overlooking Soper's Hole, called The Jolly Roger. And anyone who has tried brunch at The Tamarind Club in Josiah's Bay will almost certainly rave about it. And everyone, *everyone*, should drop by Egbert Donovan's North Shore Shell Museum in Carrot Bay.

There are places where good food and music blend together perfectly: Myett's on Cane Garden Bay, and the incomparable Quito's Gazebo where our good friend Quito provides beautiful acoustic music twice a week and then entertains again with his amazing band on Fridays and Saturdays.

Want basic? Check out the cheeseburger at Stanley's Welcome Bar—the very sandwich that inspired Jimmy Buffett to pen "Cheeseburger in Paradise" (he told me so himself). By the way, check out the spelling on the T-shirts they sell there.

Want lobster? From Tortola to Jost Van Dyke and Anegada, the search for the perfect crustacean in paradise may be reason enough to travel to Latitude 18.

In fact, the biggest problem in the BVI's these days is just where to go! I hope this book helps you find the perfect meal in paradise. Bon Appétit!

Malcolm Boyes, author of Tales of the Tropics
Little Apple Bay, Tortola

Preface

When most people hear the name BVI, they immediately think "Yachting Capital of the World." Yet, with Anegada lobster, local conch, fresh papaya, mango, and passion fruit galore, the British Virgin Islands are beginning to define themselves as far more than sunshine and placid waters. In fact, the BVI's are home to some of the best local ingredients and recipes in all of the Caribbean.

Most of the fertile land in the islands is found on hill slopes at higher elevations as well as in the valleys. With a rotational method of cultivation, local farmers alternate from food crops to pasture, peddling their harvest directly to the consumer or to local markets scattered throughout the islands.

What does this mean for you?

It means no freezing or transporting of goods for 2,500 miles or more. Instead, shoppers are treated to wonderful and unusual varieties that they'll never find in supermarkets back home. Best of all, these hometown goodies can be sampled at the height of their freshness, usually within twenty-four hours of being harvested.

The Minister of Natural Resources and Labor in the BVI's, encourages locals and visitors alike to focus on produce from BVI farmers and purveyors. While the territory is partly dependent on imported food to satisfy the varied palates of tourists, the real flair of the islands is found when venturing inward to discover fragrant tropical gardens and exotic fruits on the hillsides.

The islands are finally receiving recognition for their agriculture as a result of recent honors awarded to the BVI National Culinary Team, masters of cooking with only the freshest of local ingredients. Headed by Wilford "Willo" Stoutt, executive chef at Peter Island, the culinary team demonstrated many varieties of local recipes to over two thousand hoteliers from thirty-two Caribbean countries at a recent competition.

Many visitors are discovering that produce that is locally grown by small farmers not only tastes better, but is also more nutritious and less likely to be contaminated by pesticides than imported products. Local fruit and produce, with more vitamins and minerals, have an extra zip and are tastier, as evidenced by the number of BVI restaurants now supporting local farmers and using ingredients indigenous to the islands on their menus.

The demand is there, and it's no wonder.

Take a step outside, or take a hike through the Sage Mountain National Park on Tortola. What do you see? There is fruit wherever you look. Mangoes, breadfruit, and coconuts are just the beginning.

Many tropical trees, such as the mango tree, are cultivated for their large, oval, smooth-skinned fruit that has a juicy aromatic pulp. Island fare such as this can be found in everything from salads to desserts, and just about everything in between. Locals find the sweet and sour tang of mango chutneys to be the perfect complement to a roti—an East Indian crepe-like wrap filled with meat or vegetables and available at restaurants throughout the islands. Similarly, with melon-sized breadfruit abounding throughout the BVI's, it should come as no surprise that such natural treats pop up in almost every "down home" recipe. Used most often in savory and sweet dishes, breadfruit can be served undercooked and grated in a skillet as hash browns, mashed with butter and coconut cream like potatoes, or served as a fritter in the style of a French croquette. With ample helpings of fiery jerk recipes, the slightly bland taste of breadfruit provides a nice balance to many island entrees.

Tropical fruits aside, the BVI's also produce a variety of vegetables due to its hearty soil and climate. Vegetable gardens, like sweet potato fields, are abundant and free of borers found in other countries due to a common trick used among islanders, involving banana stems covered with honey. Crops grown without pesticides create a sustainable agricultural system which is perfect for those who can't get enough of treats like sweet potato pudding, a popular island recipe. Calling for everything local—from homegrown pumpkins, tannia, and sweet potato to grated coconut, and nutmeg—sweet potato pudding is not to be missed. Dressed up, the sweet potato is also a favorite to chefs at fine dining establishments, who often combine sweet potatoes with seared red snapper or yellowfin tuna caught by local fishermen.

Freshly baked bread is a must for any good meal. In BVI, many locals opt for cassava flour, cultivated throughout the tropical world as a substitute to wheat and other imported flour. Cassava preparations can be tedious as peeling, soaking, cutting, pounding, and drying are involved. Yet, one can hardly argue with the sweetness of the end result. Cassava bread, often served by the tray-loads, is perfect for dove pork and is best when used to soak up liqueurs or marinades left over on a plate.

Any review of the culinary arts of the BVI's would be remiss if it did not mention the plentiful gifts from the sea. From grilled whelk on the topside of a wire rack to the hush puppy quality of conch fritters, the BVI's are blessed with many nautical ingredients. Lobster receives most of the fanfare, generally synonymous with Anegada, and is often served over an open fire by local chefs. Unlike the frozen dark red lobster with large claws found in many restaurant chains, Caribbean Spiny Lobster is found at relatively shallow depths under coral heads right here in the BVI's. Caught the day it arrives on your plate, local chefs never allow the lobster to die, which would cause the potent enzymes in the digestive tract to decompose the meat. Absolute freshness is a must, and many chefs will even arrange for the fresh lobster to be grilled on your own private beach with locally-made charcoal.

Cooking in the islands is naturally influenced by its surroundings, thus seafood is prepared in every shape and form. A long-time favorite of islanders is a Caribbean version of gumbo, known fondly as Callaloo. Locals pick only the healthiest of green dasheen leaves (identifiable by a large purple dot) and ripe vegetables to add to the long simmering stew. Often, Caribbean eggplant and okra are added as thickening agents to the garlic, scallions, thyme, and Scotch bonnet peppers. Freshly caught whole crabs and lobster cut in medallions top this simple, yet tasty, island creation.

Surrounded by the island's bounty, there are obviously many reasons to buy and eat local produce. In today's global marketplace, we rarely get the chance to see what is behind the stuff we buy. Where does it come from? What are the working conditions for the people who created it? What kinds of chemicals were used?

In the BVI's this simply isn't the case. Look above, below, and around you. It's all there. Nature's best recipes are right at your fingertips.

Keep that in mind come dinnertime.

LET'S BEGIN WITH A LIL' HISTORY

The first inhabitants of the British Virgin Islands—the Arawak, Carib, and Taino Indians—contributed greatly to today's culinary melting pot of recipes, cooking methods, and local ingredients.

From the Arawaks, we have what is today affectionately known as barbeque—an Indian cooking method that uses a grate made of green wood strips. Meat cooked slowly over this grate, known as barbecue, produced the wonderful wood-smoke flavor we love today.

The Carib Indians, quite possibly having the most impact on early Caribbean cooking, were masters with spices. First adding lemon and lime juice to their fish recipes, the Caribs eventually came to discover spice—hot pepper sauces in particular.

The Taino, not to be forgotten, were the first chefs to cook fresh fish and meat in large clay pots. Also masters at selecting local fruits, the Taino knew to select the very best papaw, guava, and cassava.

The culinary arts of the islands continued to evolve once Europeans brought Africans into the region as slaves. Blending traditional African recipes with local ingredients found in abundance on the islands, slaves used their creativity to invent tasty pudding, souse, and callaloo.

Once slavery was abolished, more cooking styles were continuously introduced as Europeans looked towards India and China for labor. Curry and kari podi from India were introduced into the recipes, along with such staples as rice from China, and a variety of fruits from Spain and Portugal.

Eventually, American chefs added beans, corn, potatoes, and tomatoes to the Caribbean diet, solidifying island cooking as a true blend of cultures that has placed the BVI's at the culinary crossroads of the world.

Today the many chefs and cooking enthusiasts throughout the British Virgin Islands dish up an array of local tastes and traditions. In fact, BVI now offers just about every tasty food find that you can imagine. With the influx of tourists over the years, imported goods have naturally made their way to supermarket shelves and restaurant menus in order to please a variety of palates. However, to taste the real flair of the islands, opting for local produce and goodies, rather than imported foods, is the clear choice. Islanders and tourists alike know that by choosing locally grown goods, you are voting for freshness, better taste, conservation of fuel resources, and the economic viability of the local BVI community. If you look closely, locally grown treats can be found in many BVI markets and restaurants. Buying local offers not only a tastier product, but one that is less likely to be contaminated with pesticides, additives, and food enhancers. And best of all, by eating healthier local foods, you're simultaneously supporting the people who are taking care of the British Virgin Islands for future generations.

The British Virgin Islands — the culinary crossroads of the world.

Chapter 1

The Island's Bounty

• SCORE SOME CONCH HERE:

◇ Try conch pasta in a parsley sauce at the Sugar Mill on Virgin Gorda.

◇ Stuffed in mushrooms, conch takes center stage at the Callaloo Restaurant.

◇ Myett's has the best conch chowder around.

◇ Jolly Roger makes a mean stewed conch.

◇ Don't miss the conch stuffed ravioli (with banana-lemon chutney) at Tradewinds Restaurant.

◇ Some of the freshest conch in all of the islands is found at Quito's Gazebo.

◇ Healthy conch salads at Sebastian's on the Beach can't be beat.

◇ Stroll up from the beach and munch on one of the best conch fritter recipes at the Soggy Dollar Bar on Jost Van Dyke.

Trendsetter Tip:

Try making fritters out of breadfruit, eggplant, sweet potato, or okra. The contrast of the slightly mushy inside is highlighted by the perfectly golden fried outer shell.

While the trendy pressure cookers used in many kitchens today are handy, some islanders simply bypass them and "pound it out" by hand. Others tenderize conch meat by rubbing it with a papaya leaf.

  CONCH FRITTERS

Ingredients:
1 cup conch meat, chopped (about ½ pound)
½ cup lime juice
1 quart oil for frying
¾ cup all-purpose flour
1 egg, beaten
½ cup milk
Ground cayenne pepper to taste
Seasoned salt to taste
Local salt and pepper to taste
½ onion, chopped
½ green bell pepper, chopped
2 stalks celery, chopped
2 cloves, garlic, chopped fine
1 teaspoon lime juice

Locals Do It Like This:
Clean the tasty conch thoroughly and make sure that only the sweet white conch flesh is used. Pound away at it -- tenderizing the conch meat until it's ¼-inch thick -- is the only way! Dice the conch meat into a minimum of ¼-inch cubes. Marinate the conch with the lime juice for thirty minutes. In a bowl, mix the flour, egg, and milk – then add seasoned salt, salt, cayenne pepper, and pepper to taste. Next, finely chop and combine the onion, pepper, garlic, and celery. Add the marinated conch meat to the mixture, making sure to discard the lime juice. Fold everything together to form a thick dough, then cover and refrigerate for one hour. Preheat a deep fryer to 365 degrees F. Remove the dough and let stand for 15 minutes. Shape fritters into balls (don't flatten) and spoon into hot oil. Fry until golden brown. Drain the fritters on paper towels and serve immediately with fresh lemon or lime wedge.

Caribbean Sauce:
Ingredients:
½ cup mayonnaise
2 tbsp tomato ketchup
¼ cup chopped onion
¼ cup sweet pickle relish
½ tbsp Scotch Bonnet sauce (Cow Wreck Bar suggests Matouk's Calypso Hot Sauce)

Locals Do It Like This:
Mix the sauce ingredients. To make it unforgettable, add more Scotch bonnet sauce. Make sure to serve fritters with sauce for dipping.

THE FAMOUS FRITTER

Arguably the most talked about culinary creation ever to cross the kitchen table in the British Virgin Islands, conch fritters may resemble the humble hush puppy but they play ball in an entirely different park.

Conch, when tenderized properly, can easily become your most talked about island appetizer, entrée, or sustaining life force. Often called "Stamp and Go" when made with salt fish in other Caribbean locations, BVIslanders know the secret to the perfect fritter is using the freshest conch, as well as the right breading mixture that doesn't absorb too much oil.

So what is all the fuss really about?

Pronounced conk, this edible mollusk, in a pretty pink shell, is an island delight and is served in many ways—conch chowder, pâté, conch salad, and stewed conch. And when tenderized, chopped, and made into tasty fritters the world can't get enough of them. In fact, conch fritters have become so popular that they now suffer from over-collection.

Make sure to try conch fritters with your favorite island beverage, as it's the best snack companion to cocktails! And, like oysters, conch is often rumored to be one of the world's best aphrodisiacs.

Courtesy of Soggy Dollar Bar

After feasting on conch fritters and tropical cocktails, patrons of The Soggy Dollar Bar spend the rest of the day limin' in a beachside hammock.

• FOR THE CONCH PURIST:

If you're a conch purist, then go with straight-up conch meat that has been tenderized. Marinate in lime juice and a sprinkle or two of salt. Fresh conch doesn't need all the fixings.

• FOR THE CONCH TOURIST:

Conch should be white with pinkish-orange edges. If it's grayish in color, avoid it. Like all seafood, it should not smell fishy. Make sure to trim any dark pieces of skin. Conch meat should have a mild, sweet clam-like flavor. The most common uses of conch are for fritters, chowder, conch steaks and marinated raw conch salad. Scungilli and whelk are distant relatives of the mighty conch.

• FOR ALL THINGS CONCH:

Head over to the family-run Cow Wreck Beach Bar and Grill (284-495-8047) for the freshest local conch creations around. Don't forget to try the Wreck Punch, made with a special blend of cane rum.

FOR ALL THINGS TORCHWOOD:

When barbecuing in the BVI, do it the local way by using Anegadan "torchwood." This dense local wood lights easily and burns for extended periods of time without turning to ash. Best of all, torchwood from Anegada has a distinctive island flavor.

 CONCH CEVICHE

Ingredients:
Fresh conch meat (2 average size conches)
½ fresh pineapple, peeled and chopped
½ cup water
1 lemon, juiced
1 lime, juiced
1 onion, chopped
1 tomato, chopped
1 cup fresh cilantro, chopped
Salt and freshly ground pepper to taste
¼ Scotch bonnet, seeded and minced (optional)

Locals Do It Like This:
As always, clean the conch meat and only use the sweet white conch. Pound gently, and then pound some more. Conch is best when it's tenderized and no more than ¼ inch thick. Dice the tasty conch meat into cubes. In a large bowl, mix together the conch, lime and lemon juice, water, cilantro, onion, pineapple, tomato, and salt. Let stand for one hour before serving. Some islanders like to serve ceviche with fresh gourmet crackers, dipping corn chips, or fresh tortillas.

 GRILLED RUM RUNNER LOBSTER

Ingredients:
1 live Anegada lobster
½ pound of butter (or 1 cup combo of butter and olive oil)
½ cup local rum
Loads of garlic, chopped
Fresh basil
Juice of 2 local key limes

Locals Do It Like This:
Combine all ingredients to create the rum butter sauce. Next, heat up your grill or beachside BBQ, and split the fresh lobster vertically from head to tail. Place shell side down on grill and baste liberally with rum butter sauce while cooking. The lobster meat will turn white when done. Different lobster and heat of grill will vary cooking times—just don't overcook. Finally, transfer the lobster to plates and sprinkle with chopped parsley or cilantro.

Courtesy of Cynthia Rose

HOOK, LINE, AND SINKER

Deep Sea Fishing: Propelling itself out of the water ("tailwalking") at ninety miles an hour, the blue marlin often fills the air in the BVI's. With world-class deep-sea fishing in abundance, those familiar with the British Virgin Islands know to look for underwater canyons that form just below plateaus.

Take for instance Anegada's North Drop and Virgin Gorda's Sound Drop. Both serve as a cobalt blue oasis for anglers and game fish alike. Dumping two hundred yards, with forty-pound strike drag, fishing enthusiasts search for "the man in the blue suit," otherwise known as the Atlantic blue marlin.

Locals tell stories of snagging four hundred pound marlin in the Biras Creek International Fishing Tournament, where boats such as the "Escape" are rumored to have caught at least eighty-seven blue marlin in one competition alone.

And the fun doesn't stop there; Wahoo, sailfish, yellowfin, marlin, blackfin tuna, dorado, and kingfish are also in abundance. In fact, locals insist that an eight-year-old boy even caught a 365-pound marlin not long ago!

Inshore Fishing: With miles and miles of reef, Anegada is naturally ringed with the incredible fighting bonefish which is perfect for the inshore fisherman. In fact, a community of anglers, some even venturing out in sea kayaks, can be spotted hovering atop other honey holes such as that of Colquhoun Reef and Eustatia Reef (near Oil Nut Bay) in the North Sound as well. Another good spot: don't miss the tiny lucky stretch just west of the Beef Island bridge, dropping a line right in the channel!

Sailing and Fishing: What could be better? Drop your line from the rear of a boat—the BVI's waters will reward you with lots of surface action. Don't be surprised: at the end of your line you're likely to find surface-munching fish like kingfish, tuna, and Spanish mackerel. Also, be on the look out for swordfish, tuna, spearfish, wahoo, and mahi-mahi. *Note: Always obtain a Temporary Fishing Permit or Sport License.*

Catch of the Day by Lisa Remeny

Reef Fishing: Be advised before you dish up, ask a local! Tropical food poisoning, also known as "ciguatera," can be found in many predatory fish around reefs. Think twice before digging into jacks, puffer fish, and some large size barracuda (which stink, by the way).

Also, don't be fooled by the triggerfish. There are three varieties, as well as a handful of sister fish such as trunkfish and boxfish—some of which are poisonous. Locals steer clear of the black triggerfish, but often turn the dark ones into a favorite dish called "'Ole Wife." Lastly, if you see a yellow one, make sure to release it—it's the rarest, and a very exotic queen fish!

Fly Fishing: One of the fastest growing sports in the world is catching fish "on the fly." In BVI it's clear why there has been a marked increase in fly fishing, as Bonefish, Permit, and Tarpon are easily scored at any number of untapped flats and reefs in the area. For your best bet, try Anegada for a shot at the "silver ghosts" of the flats.

Fishing Tips: Consider using small baitfish, feather hoochies, or ballyhoo. Locals typically use small skiffs to explore the many nooks and crannies of BVI.

Looking for Conch: Browse the sandy areas near the countless grass beds in the BVI's to find this tasty snail! Born a half-million strong, this Caribbean sensation buries itself in the sand by day and comes out at night to munch on seagrasses. A toenail-like trapdoor is the conch's method of mobility, propelling it at a slow, but steady pace. A favorite food of locals, the Queen Conch can be found in seashells up to a foot long! With commercial fishermen and starfish (a natural predator) closing in, the queen conch is a threatened species. Please note; conch collecting is strictly prohibited among tourists.

Best Times to Catch the Big Ones: BVI fishing legends insist that you'll snag wahoo and tuna year round. From September through June, you'll want to target marlin; and from October to June, start chasing the mahi-mahi. You'll most likely be bringing home wahoo as well as mahi-mahi from October through April.

The Fly Fisherman's Survival Gear: All you'll need is a nine-weight rod and a handful of Gotchas, Clousers, and Charlies.

Fishing on Beef Island: Yes, you can practically begin fishing just after stepping off the plane on Beef Island. Just north of the bridge, anglers can find a large flat that can be reached by foot or by boat (recommended). If you're not having any luck, wade out to the grass-bottom flat, south of Sprat Point in Trellis Bay.

Fishing on Guana Island: If you're looking for tarpon, head to Monkey Point on the southern tip of Guana Island (boat required).

Fishing in Sea Cows Bay (Tortola): A superb flat next to the Pieces of Eight apartment complex.

Fishing in Maya Cove (Tortola): Drop a line near the cargo barge dock, just off the main road.

Fishing Fat Hogs Bay (Tortola): East of Whale Rock, you'll want to drop a line between the island and the bushes just off Beef Island (boat required).

Fishing West End (Tortola): For tarpon and bonefish, try the small bridge (both sides) that separates Frenchman's Cay from Tortola.

Fishing on Anegada: Known as ground zero for BVI flat fishing, you won't want to miss a crack at the eleven-mile-long flat stretches along the south coast.

Fishing Jost Van Dyke: For bonefish, you'll want to try the shallows between Little Jost Van Dyke island and Jost Van Dyke island.

THE LAST SALT BARON

They say "No man is an island." Then again, they probably never met Norwell Durant.

The famous passage, made popular by the English metaphysical poet, John Donne, speaks of the belief that human beings cannot thrive when isolated from others.

Norwell Durant felt otherwise.

As the sole inhabitant of Salt Island, a tiny spit of land in the British Virgin Islands, Norwell lived alone for many years until his late seventies. In plain view, just over five miles away, he could see Tortola, the capital and hub of the British Virgin Islands, from his humble dwelling along the beachfront.

His island is simple compared to the string of nearby islands that stretch from west to east facing Tortola's southern coast. There are luxury resorts on nearby islands and tales of treasures on Norman Island, the home to Robert Louis Stevenson's classic novel. The Caribbean sun and placid waters, however, were enough for Norwell.

Many travel agents and books for tourists would have you believe that the island's only claim to fame is the "RMS Rhone," a 310-foot royal mail steamer that was split by the rocks off the coast of Salt Island in the hurricane of October 29, 1867.

The Salt Islanders at the time not only helped the handful of surviving crew from their noble vessel, but also packed up and returned all of the valuables to the Queen of England.

Over a century later, Norwell, who tended to the crews' unmarked graves, saw his home as more than just the site of the famous shipwreck.

He was a sea salt harvester—the last of his kind.

Norwell, alone, spent his days harvesting salt just as his ancestors did when the island's population reached its high of one hundred residents or so in the early 1900s. He and his family were proud of the two large evaporating salt ponds, fed by the Caribbean's Sir Frances Drake Passage, and Norwell was quick to show off the granular prize from which the island took its name.

Mostly harvesting during the dry season, Norwell, who was small in stature but with large hands and soulful brown eyes, would wade the ponds looking for depressions in the submerged salt, tediously breaking pieces from the edge. Some years had good harvests (once a thousand pounds were harvested), and others were not worth mentioning. No matter the outcome, Norwell was content.

Carrying on a tradition made popular by Queen Victoria in 1867, Norwell would leave his island once a year to offer a symbolic payment of ten pounds of salt on the queen's birthday (a health nut, she was rumored to use it regularly), an event he very much enjoyed. Aside from that, Norwell Durant spent his time watching expensive yachts from his shack with binoculars and decorating the small cemeteries on the island with shells.

Often, Norwell's cousin would take a dingy over from Tortola to keep him company and bring supplies. Though a welcomed site by the sea salt harvester, he didn't worry much about living alone.

An occasional visitor or two would happen by, sometimes a reporter or curious tourists that had heard his tale. Even celebrities, such as Morgan Freeman and Bill O'Riley, were known to spend time under a palm tree with Norwell on visits to the island. The eight member staff of nearby Cooper Island Beach Club became friends as well and were known to drop in on Norwell from time to time. His dog, Rex, was said to enjoy these types of visits most.

Eventually, Norwell gave in to prompting from his family members who feared for the aging islander's health: he moved back to Tortola. In February of 2004, the British Virgin Islands experienced treacherous rain, mudslides, and rough waters.

Norwell Durant passed away later that month.

Today, the British Virgin Islands National Park Service has preserved the old sea salt harvester's island, keeping it intact for those select few that seek out this small speck of Earth—one that has yet to be tamed, a village of shacks forgotten by civilization.

On the island, which is home to a wide range of birds and marine species—some of which are endangered or threatened in other parts of the BVI—life continues to thrive. Divers frequent the wreck of the Rhone off the coast and visitors still stop by, some wishing to sit and meditate under the palm tree where Norwell once sat. Norwell's palm tree, and the island as a whole, serves as a sanctuary that invites others to relax and leave their thoughts.

The lucky few that take a dingy over to the island are asked to heed a few simple rules. Norwell told James Anderson in an interview for the Associated Press in 2001 that everyone was welcomed. He was quoted as saying, "Behave yourself in my yard. I'm not a preacher, but have respect. Be quiet…. be happy…. that's my way."

Salt Island is 6 mi/9.7 km E of Tortola, between Peter Island (W) and Cooper Island (E), 18° 22'N 64° 30'W.

OTHER NOTABLE RESIDENTS OF SALT ISLAND:

Norwell Durant may have been the last of the famous Salt Islanders, yet there were certainly other residents that stand as testament to this special speck of earth. Clementine Helena Leonard Smith, born on May 9, 1911, was such a resident. Clementine grew up on Salt Island, and, like Norwell, left her impact. After attending elementary school in Tortola, Clementine returned to her island where she fished, tended to livestock, and mined for salt. She had nine children who eventually moved to nearby Tortola. Spending her days tending to the burial ground of passengers from the wreck of the Rhone, Clementine maintained the beaches and the salt ponds and welcomed the occasional tourists with bits of island folklore. Officially recognized for her efforts in 1985, Clementine received the British Empire Member Medal, and in 1996 the Frederick Pickering Memorial Foundation honored her for social and cultural contributions. Clementine died in 1998 and was buried in the graveyard that she cared for during her many years on Salt Island. Clementine's grave is marked with large stones and conch shells.

Salt Island - untouched, unspoiled, unbelievable.

LOOKING FOR BVI SALT?

Until a few years ago, local salt was harvested and sold by the lone salt baron on Salt Island in the BVI's. Surprisingly to some, salt-based curing and seasoning is still practiced in the British Virgin Islands. Many locals will make seasoned salt recipes by grinding salt with garlic cloves, celery, parsley, black pepper, onion, nutmeg, and thyme for an amazing dry marinade.

THE MOST WELL-KNOWN SALT POND:

Sure, BVI has numerous salt ponds dotting its many islands, but Salt Island is the most famous of them all. In fact, no other island in BVI has produced more salt than this small T-shaped island that for centuries was home to a settlement of sea salt harvesters. At one time, up to one thousand pounds of salt was harvested annually from Salt Island.

BREAKING OF THE POND:

During early spring, at the end of the dry season, the water in the two shallow salt ponds on Salt Island evaporates, leaving a hard outer layer of salt along the edges of the pond. In years gone by, a festival, attended by the BVI governor and members of the Royal BVI police, was held to mark the occasion. Many BVIslanders traveled to Salt Island to take part in the annual "breaking of the pond" harvesting party. After the fun, the salt was harvested from the pond and dried in a salt house.

LIFE BEFORE TOURISM:

Salt Island has no electricity, no ferry service, and now, no residents. Strolling along the north coast you'll find only coconut palms and a handful of empty homes peppering the landscape. Life here is simple and free of tourism and large scale development. Visitors to this tiny speck of earth will want to hike the trails circling the pond, as well as explore South Bay in the west and the Sound in the east.

THE WRECK OF THE RHONE:

Salt Island's claim to fame, the Rhone, is one of the most popular dive sites in all of the British Virgin Islands. Diving the Rhone, which is still in good condition, provides a gander at an abundance of fish and coral. The Rhone rests on a reef in twenty to eighty feet of water, so snorkeling is an excellent option. Diving the Rhone is certainly recommended. Head to the deeper bow section of the boat and you might recognize some of the famous scenes from the movie The Deep. You'll also want to follow the anchor line down and explore part of the mast and the hull. Keep an eye out for the water pump, the boiler, the "lucky porthole," the silver spoon, and the prop and rudder. Swimming inside the wreck, you'll be greeted by colorful schools of parrotfish, snapper, soldier fish, grunts, and if you're lucky, the queen angelfish.

RHONE—QUICK FACTS:

- 310-foot Royal Mail Steamship: one of the first iron ships built.
- On October 29, 1867, the Rhone arrived at Peter Island and anchored off Dead Man's Bay. When a hurricane descended upon the Rhone, the anchor dragged and broke free from its holding.
- The Rhone now lies broken into two pieces beneath twenty to eighty feet of water and is encrusted with colorful coral.
- Approximately 120 passengers and crew perished, including Captain Robert F. Wooley. Approximately twenty-five survived.
- Salt Island villagers recovered eight bodies from the water.
- Several years after the wreck, divers salvaged twenty thousand dollars worth of gold and money, along with copper and liquor, before the National Parks Trust preserved the wreck.

CONCH STEW (ALSO CALLED CONCH PIE)

Ingredients:
5 lbs conch meat
2 tsp black pepper
3 strips bacon, crispy and crushed
2 tbsp Ketchup (If you can get your hands on it, try Pickapeppa. Often called "Jamaican Ketchup," this sweet flavored sauce was created in Shooter's Hill, Jamaica in 1921)
5 to 6 cups coconut water (from 2 to 3 coconuts)
3 tbsp margarine
2 green peppers, chopped
2 tsp thyme
3 onions
Salt to taste

Locals Do It Like This:
As always, pound the conch very well. And then pound it again! Slice the conch, placing it into a cooking pot. Cover with coconut water and bring to a boil. Simmer for 20 minutes or until tender.

Mix in pepper, bacon, green bell peppers, thyme, onions, and cook for 40 minutes. Add "pie" (tiny dumplings) on top, and simmer until cooked. To create the "pie," use 2 cups flour, water, and salt until you have formed a dough that is easy to knead and form into dumplings. Add a touch of tomato ketchup, or Pickapeppa Sauce.

WHERE ARE THE HONEY HOLES?

Let these hometown guides show you …

- Pelican Charters: Captain Tim Fish—yes, that's really his name—can arrange deep sea adventures out of Prospect Reef Resorts. To hop a ride on the Whopper, call 284-496-7386.

- Princess: Captain Dale, bustin' out of Biras Creek on a thirty-one foot Bertram, is one of the best in the sport fishing business. Reach him if you can at 284-495-7248.

- The Bitter End: Expect in the ballpark of $400 for a full day, but what you'll get is a twenty-six foot speedboat that is equipped for every angling scenario imaginable (284-494-2746).

- Caribbean Fly Fishing: For some high-stakes bonefishing action, try 284-499-1590.

- Sea It All: This thirty foot Mappy Bertram is known for almost guaranteed deep sea fishing success (284495-7558).

- Cadie's Fishing Trips: A jack of all trades, try this small yet powerful 17' Boston Whaler for just about any fishing romp you can imagine (284-499-3853).

- Need some equipment? Head on over to Richardson's Rigging (284-494-2739) or Little Denmark, both of which are found in Road Town.

- How about a fishing permit? It'd be a good idea to call the Fisheries Division (284-494-3429) before you drop a line.

- Anegada Reef Hotel: If you're looking for a serious fishing vacation, then head to the waters around Anegada and drop your bags off at the Anegada Reef Hotel (284-495-8002). It offers a wealth of fishing charters and can arrange deep-sea charters to boot.

- Ask Garfield: While on Anegada you'll want to seek out Garfield's Guides (284-495-9569 or 284-4996374) as well. These fine folks provide some of the best bonefishing tours in BVI.

- Caribbean Fly Fishing: Located in Nanny Cay Marina, Caribbean Fly Fishing (284-494-4797 or 284-4991590) prides itself on taking you to "un-fished flats" and reefs teeming with bonefish, permit, and tarpon. Check 'em out online at www.caribflyfishing.com.

- Big Ting Fishing Charters: Big Ting (284-499-2837), on Virgin Gorda, boasts a 42-foot Bertram that is known to participate in the top fishing tournaments in the Leeward Islands. In fact, Big Ting has become such the rage that this is the very boat that carries the ESPN World Wide Fishing Team with Captain Norman Isaac.

STRAY, STRAY FROM THE BEATEN PATH

- Stray from the beaten path. Only footsteps away from anchoring cruise ships, you'll find extensive flats, an ideal spot for game fish—tarpon, barracuda, bonefish, and jacks. Fishermen diving for conch or whelk just north of the salt ponds are also a common sight.

- Hop a ride with a local or flag down a cab to explore the extreme hills around Tortola and the many hidden coves and beaches.

- Head to the ferry docks for a ride over to the Bitter End Resort. Whether you are a guest or not, you'll enjoy a buffet of island goodies.

- If you are not in the mood for fancy cocktails and regattas, then get off at the next stop, which is Gun Creek on Virgin Gorda. There you can schmooze with locals, such as Bozo, at the tiny "Last Stop" bar. A local hometown hero who is always telling tales at the open-air pub, Bozo will happily shoot the breeze for hours if you buy him a drink.

- Consider one of the many private chefs that the British Virgin Islands have to offer. Martha Collymore, for example, also known as "Chef Mimi," is a private dinner chef in Virgin Gorda. Popular for her classic Caribbean cuisine, Chef Mimi routinely impresses fans with her three-course menu ($65 per person) including such treats as conch fritters, pumpkin soup, Anegada lobster, grilled fish with Creole sauce, and coconut cream cake. To contact Chef Mimi, give Tropical Care Services a ring, 284-495-6493, or email info@tropicalcareservices.com.

- Explore the many tiny shops, open-air markets, and side streets, especially in Road Town and West End at Soper's Hole, looking for local art, handmade jewelry, dolls, calabash bags, and straw hats. The mood is friendly and you may even stumble into a steel band.

- When your feet get tired, but you're still serious about exploring hidden gems, snag a good cabbie, or get your own ride. Look for taxis on Beef Island, Wickham's Cay, near the ferry dock in Road Town and Soper's Hole—or call the BVI Taxi Association (284-494-2875). If you're on Virgin Gorda, taxis can be found easily at the airport or at the Yacht Harbour ferry dock. A ride to anywhere in The Valley should run approximately $3, with the cost rising to around $20 when heading to Gun Creek. You may also want to ring one of the fine taxi services and rental businesses–such as Speedy's (284-495-5240), Andy's Jeep Rentals (284-495-5252), L&S Garage Taxi & Car Rental (284-495-5297), or Mahogany Rentals and Taxi Service (284-495-5469).

- After you've taken in the real flair of the British Virgin Islands, consider tapping into what really makes it tick—philanthropy. Over a period of years starting in the 1960s, the late Laurance Rockefeller defined the spirit of giving, as evidenced by the more than 200 acres he donated to the National Parks Trust. Today this kind of generosity can still be witnessed, seen in many local businesses and churches throughout the islands. While visiting, consider offering your time—or simply a pat on the back—to such do-gooders as the BVI Reading Council, Animal Rescue and Control of Virgin Gorda, Youth Empowerment Programme, Virgin Gorda Youth Initiative, Red Cross, Human Society, and the Diabetes Association.

Cow Wreck Bay

 LOBSTER CHOWDER

Ingredients:
1 ½ cups Anegada lobster meat
1 potato
1 cup water
2 tsp butter
1 onion
1 tsp BVI salt
½ tsp paprika
½ tsp white pepper
2 cups milk
1 cup light cream
2 tbsp cognac
Fresh parsley

Locals Do It Like This:
Peel and dice the potatoes and mix with water and salt in a saucepan. Bring the mixture to a boil, and then remove from heat and set aside. Mince the onion and sauté it in the butter in the saucepan. Stir in the seasonings, and then add the milk and cream. Bring to a boil. Reduce the heat to a simmer and continue to stir. Next, chop the lobster and add it to the smooth mixture. Stir, and add the potatoes. Continue to simmer for an additional 10 minutes and then add the cognac. Add the fresh parsley before serving!

BEST PLACE FOR CARIBBEAN LOBSTER:

The votes are in, and the obvious winner is Anegada! Most pick Cow Wreck Beach Bar & Grill, but any of a handful of local eateries will leave your mouth watering for more. If you want to spot some "big bugs" in the wild, then take a peak under protected crevices (rocks and coral heads) for this spiny variety which, by the way, lacks claws. Look for the lobster's large antennas sticking out from its hiding place. If you see one, there'll probably be more hiding nearby.

WHERE ARE THE BEST BIG BUGS?

- For Lobster On Anegada:
  Anegada Reef Hotel—barbecued for dinner
  Big Bamboo—boiled for lunch

- For Lobster on Virgin Gorda:
  Giorgio's Table—served Catalana style
  Bitter End Clubhouse— Lobster Bahamian

- For Lobster On Jost Van Dyke:
  Sydney's Peace and Love
  Abe's By the Sea
  Harris' Place

WHAT'S FISH ADOBO?

This age old recipe (a national dish of the Philippines) is perfect for any fish worth frying. In other words, it's a perfect recipe for cooking on a boat or beachside BBQ.

Locals in BVI say this recipe works best with snapper, tilapia, or halibut. Add a little adobo criollo seasoning or any good seasoning salt, and this one really pops!

Well known BVI travelers and kitchen phenoms, Nancy and Walker from www.bvipirate.com, insist that a heavy amount of Bohio seasoning sin pimiento will also do the trick. As the operators of one of the most popular BVI information clearinghouses, Nancy and Walker have found that Bohio seasoning is what makes this recipe work. If you haven't discovered it, find it! Bohio is from Puerto Rico and is found just about anywhere in the British Virgin Islands. If you can't score some Bohio, then seek out adobo criollo seasoning which is just as tasty. For more tasty ideas, check out www.bvipirate.com.

Once you've found a good stash of seasoning that is to your liking, apply it to your fresh catch immediately before the fish is placed in a skillet. Make sure the tasty seasoning forms a light crust as the fish cooks. Be sure not to apply the seasoning too soon—as the fish stands the moisture will dissolve the seasoning, and you'll have an extremely salty dish on your hands.

WHERE DO VEGETARIANS EAT IN BVI?

With all the chatter over local fish, conch, lobster, and goat, veggie lovers might be wondering what's in it for them. The quick answer is quite simple—take your pick. BVI is loaded with such versatile fruits as mangoes, which make their way into everything from stir-fries to frozen drinks, as well as chayote (also called christophene), popping up in everything from soup to pancakes. Likewise, plantains are a popular option, served roasted, sautéed, or added to unbeatable stews. And who says going veg can't be daring, as spicy sancocho, an unbeatable vegetable stew with plantains, really kicks. Local BVI eateries, such as Garden Restaurant (284-495-4931) at Carrot Bay on Tortola, are known for creative vegetarian dishes. Vegetarians will also want to seek out Nature's Way (284-494-6393) on the North Shore.

WHY EAT BVI LOCAL?

For one, locally grown BVI food just tastes better, as it was most likely picked within the past day or two. It's crisp, sweet, and loaded with flavor. In other words, it comes to you ripe and fresh, unlike supermarket food that may have been picked months before. In addition, local BVI produce is better for you and is GMO-free. And best of all, local BVI food supports local farm families and builds community. When you buy direct from the farmer, you are reestablishing a time-honored connection. In short, local eating is social. Shopping at BVI farmers' markets provides locals and tourists alike a greater likelihood for more conversations and opportunity to learn about the locality, its foods, and its people.

BOMBA SHACK

It's a time to break bad habits and bad addictions. Every twenty-eight and a half days the full moon reaches its zenith, a time that some say is well-suited for spells that can transform lives and increase psychic abilities.

Or in Bomba's case, just an excuse for one hell of a good time.

Bomba's Surfside Shack, a colorful mixture of plywood and clapboard on a picturesque bay in Tortola, is home to one of the largest full moon parties in the world.

Hundreds of local residents, sunburned surfers, wealthy yacht owners, Rastafarians, European backpackers, and tourists fresh off of cruise ships, all rub elbows with this larger-than-life legend, known simply as Bomba.

Wall-to-wall people jammed into a tiny shack that looks like it's going to collapse at any minute makes the Bomba Shack a place that is not to be missed.

At midnight partygoers can expect to find the slightly disheveled man under a large palm tree across the street. Stirring a large black kettle, Bomba, with a thick beard and gold rim glasses, lovingly boils water over a fire in preparation for his mushroom tea.

This mighty concoction contains psychedelic mushrooms, natural wonders that pop up after a rainfall. Each party's recipe is slightly different, yet all contain a small to medium dose of chopped 'shrooms and other secret ingredients that Bomba is sure not to disclose. Locals and tourists alike often search the Sage Mountain Mini Rain Forest on Tortola, looking for a bumper crop of island mushrooms to make their own mixtures.

The 'shroom itself, with a dark stripe around the stem, is not illegal in Tortola. Selling it, on the other hand, gets tricky, depending on who you ask. Skirting the issue, in a perfectly acceptable fashion, Bomba sells large mugs (for ten bucks a pop) so that his guests may partake of the free beverage throughout the night.

Tea or no tea, the shack itself is worth a visit. Undies, everything from lacy thongs to your grandmother's bloomers, hang from the ceiling and blow in the balmy winds under the tin roof structure.

Bomba is quick to offer up free T-shirts and drinks to ladies willing to trade an item of their own clothing, a challenge many guests are not afraid to take up. Polaroid pictures of women exposing their breasts adorn the colorful walls.

With Bomba's punch in hand, a tamer version of the mushroom elixir, some bypass the full moon hoopla and head down on a Wednesday or Sunday night when there's live music and a mean barbecue to enjoy.

No matter the night you visit the shack, there's sure to be a party that is unlikely to stop, no matter the time or even the threat of a hurricane. In fact, Bomba's Shack has been completely demolished by more than one hurricane (Hurricane Marilyn was among the worst). Each time it's miraculously hammered back together by fans the very next day.

♫ BOMBA-QUICK FACTS:

- Bomba built his famous shack along the sandy beach in Cappoons Bay (beside Apple Bay) in 1976.
- Bomba's digs are made mostly of surfboards, driftwood, and pieces of tin roofing.
- Bomba's Shack has always proven popular with surfers in nearby Apple Bay.
- Bomba hosted his first full-moon party in 1989, an event that continues to build in popularity to this day.
- Bomba's parties take place right on the road, between Bomba's two buildings.
- Bomba's shindigs are best known for live music, dancing, free T-shirts, and his mythical mushroom concoctions.

SALT FISH:

Back in the day, locals would use salt to preserve food on long romps at sea. British Virgin Islanders, who generally opt for cod but sometimes munch on mackerel, have perfected the art of salt fish as a main course. The best of the best salt fish in the islands can be found near the roundabout at the top of Main Street. Known as Virgin Queen (284-429-2310), this local eatery has a large carryout business due to its reputation for preparing only the best local cooking around. Though their stewed mutton and doved pork alone is worth the trip, the real draw is this hot spot's popular salt fish. To score your first taste, head to Fleming Street near the roundabout.

SAVE IT FOR LATER:

If you're boat cooking and want to save these treats for later, make sure to freeze them in a sealed container or refrigerate them in a plastic bag. They're just as good reheated, but don't let them sit around for too long!

DA ISLAND'S BEST SALT FISH CAKE (ALSO KNOWN AS STAMP AND GO)

Ingredients:
2 tbsp oil (locals use coconut oil)
1 cup onions, finely chopped
1 cup of flour
1 tsp baking powder
1 egg, lightly beaten
¾ cup milk
1 tbsp butter, melted of course
2 tbsp onions or eschalots, chop, chop, chop—until very fine. (Many locals agree, using eschalots instead of onions works best as the flavor is a bit milder and complements this dish well)
½ lb, salted cod fish, soaked, skinned, cooked, drained, and flaked
1 hot pepper—make sure it's fresh and finely chopped.
Salt and pepper to taste

Locals Do It Like This
Marinate the salt fish overnight for the tastiest results. After soaking, change the water and simmer for 30 minutes before draining. Flake the fish into small pieces, and set aside.

Using a heavy frying pan, sauté the eschalot or onions in the oil until slightly wilted.

Mix the flour, baking powder, and salt together in a separate container. Locals like to hollow out a well-like tunnel in the center, and pour the egg, milk, and butter inside. Now stir it up, adding in the salted cod fish, eschalot, salt, and pepper. Use a spoon to scoop and drop a full dollop into the hot oil in the frying pan. Make sure not to overcrowd these salty beauties in the pan! Fry 'em up until golden brown and serve 'em hot.

BVI BEACHCOMBING

Searching BVI beaches for shells and other well-traveled items is a favorite pastime for many seasoned beachcombers. More than one thousand species of shells populate the many BVI beaches, including sea biscuits, starfish, whelk, jewel boxes, cowries, and helmets, to name just a few. Serious collectors will also want to stop by the North Shore Shell Museum and see the massive collection of shells and driftwood owned by master sheller Egbert Donovan. Also, make sure to stroll the following recommended beaches (just remember—do not remove any marine organisms from BVI waters):

Virgin Gorda: Explore Savannah Bay, Pond Bay, and Oil Nut Bay for a wealth of seaside finds.

Anegada: Try your luck along the southeast corner where you'll be treated to the largest heaping of conch shells in all of BVI.

Jost Van Dyke: Head straight to Diamond Cay and you'll find a hefty helping of shelling opportunities.

Tortola: Don't miss a chance to discover the wealth of shells along any of the North Shore beaches. And if you can keep a secret, head over to the south shore as well. Few know this, but strolling this section of Tortola reaps many seashells even though there are few swimmable beaches.

Peter Island: This sandy spot boasts more than 1,800 acres of lush, untainted tropical island and five beaches. Try White Bay, which can be found after a fun hike to the other side of the island away from most charterers.

Great Dog: Comb the north side for seaside treasures.

George Dog: Head to the very southeast point and you'll be rewarded with shells galore.

Guana Island: Explore the North Bay and you won't be disappointed.

Great Camanoe: North Bay is where you'll find scores of conch.

Ginger Island: This is a good stopover for beachcombing.

Cooper Island: Check out the windward side of Hallsover Bay on this tiny island paradise.

Dead Chest: Take a jaunt over to the north side to score some seaside treasures.

Salt Island: Explore the shallows and the water's edge along the beach; you won't be disappointed. When you're finished, head inward and discover the sound!

Norman Island: Try your hand at Money Bay.

COOPER ISLAND

Just about every beach resort these days brags of its private and secluded beaches. Yet another deserted island: walk for miles and see no one. Yeah, yeah, we've heard it all before.

In reality, much of this is a marketing gimmick dreamed up by some investor from the States hanging out in a hammock after too many Caribs. Having an all-inclusive resort pack lazy guests into a minivan for a touristy trip over to the other side of the island for the day just doesn't cut it.

Cooper Island in the British Virgin Islands, on the other hand, has no such public relations team. Located on Manchioneel Bay on the northwest corner, only those lucky enough to stumble upon the tiny spit of land know of it. In fact, most discover the island's existence only after a sailing trip from Tortola or while diving the sunken RMS Rhone nearby.

With no roads, no traffic, no telephone lines, and no cheesy day-trippers, the island smacks of authenticity. The population is a grand total of nine people, give or take a few. The locals are made up of a family of three that runs the Cooper Island Beach Club, and a handful of staff. Oh, and let's not forget about the numerous goats running wild along the island (which is about one and a half miles long, half a mile wide).

Nestled in a batch of palm trees on the beach are eleven guest rooms—all about fifty feet from the water's edge. They are nothing fancy; think of rattan furniture and outdoor garden showers. However, the casual atmosphere is appropriate, as the activities on the island are mostly made up of snorkeling, walking, and reading. Sailing charters, kayaks, and windjammers can be arranged but that's about the extent of the island's festivities.

What Cooper Island does offer is attentive, but discrete service, allowing guests to create their own vacation; something few large-scale resorts can claim. The fully equipped SCUBA dive center, a seventeen-year-old beachfront restaurant (try the conch fritters), and unforgettable sunset views make the destination something you might want to consider keeping a secret.

Cooper Island Beach Club is not your typical Caribbean resort—it's better.

LITTLE THATCH ISLAND

If kicking back on your own private island is your style, look no further than Little Thatch. Just south of West End Tortola, Little Thatch offers fifty-four acres to call your own. If idyllic, white sand beaches aren't enough, this private island boasts five luxury guest cottages that all lead to a handcrafted Great Room, perched atop the crest of the island. Renting Little Thatch will also give you a crack at the island's fresh water pool, a twenty-four-foot powerboat with your own captain and a discreet staff of ten.

NECKER ISLAND

If ultra-plush tropical style strikes your fancy, then Necker Island is the place for you. Part of the Virgin Limited Edition, a handful of extremely individual and luxurious properties around the world, Necker is typically hired as a whole island (though they do offer some weeks in which couples can book individual rooms as well as a "Family Fun Week" with activities designed around children). Necker Island is the extreme in private luxury—with an endless supply of beach toys and a fleet of pampering staff (fifty of them in fact) at the ready. Necker Island lies off the far north of Virgin Gorda. Locals fondly remember the days when Princess Di used to visit Necker Island, one of the few places the paparazzi couldn't reach her.

ANEGADA DAY TRIP

An Anegada Day Trip is a treat not to be missed. Out of Tortola or Virgin Gorda, Fly BVI requires a minimum of four persons (call for prices). From Virgin Gorda these flyboys typically charge $250 a pop. To make life easier, Fly BVI includes in this price not only the flight but also the taxi ride from the Anegada Airport over to Loblolly Bay beach, a lobster lunch at the Big Bamboo restaurant (depending upon availability), and the return taxi ride.

While on Anegada, you're certain to have a memorable time snorkeling, playing volleyball on the beach, lying in a hammock, or simply lazing on the white sandy beach. While there, consider working something out with your taxi driver to arrange for a tour around the island to spot flamingos and visit the local shops (this is not part of the Fly BVI package). If you prefer to rent a car while on Anegada, it's best that you arrange for the rental in advance as there are no rental agencies at the airport and they would have to deliver a car to the airport upon your arrival.

For those looking for a different route, there is now a ferry to Anegada. See reservationsbvi.com and click ferries for the latest on traveling to Anegada. Other options include a chance to ride with Captain Keith Williams on a memorable private sail aboard the famed Spirit of Anegada.

On a typical day Fly BVI departs around 9:30 am and collects you from Anegada at 4:30 pm, so that you can enjoy the entire day in Anegada. To arrange such a trip, call Fly BVI, (284-495-1747) a few days in advance and advise them of the passenger names, where you are staying while in the British Virgin Islands, the exact date you wish for your day trip, the number of passengers, and the method of payment.

OTHER BVI AIR CHARTERS   ·

Caribbean Wings: This established outfit offers air charters within the British Virgin Islands, with flights to and from Beef Island Airport (EIS)—Tortola, Virgin Gorda, Anegada, San Juan, Puerto Rico, St. Thomas (U.S. Virgin Islands), St. Maarten, St. Martin, Antigua, Anguilla, and other island destinations. Owned and operated by Captain Warren Wheeler, an experienced airline pilot, Caribbean Wings caters mostly to sailors chartering in the British Virgin Islands, and to villa renters on Virgin Gorda and Anegada. In operation since 1983, Caribbean Wings' slogan is "Flying is an art ... the Caribbean is our canvas." (284-495-6000)

Island Birds: Based at Beef Island Airport, Island Birds offers private flights throughout the Caribbean. (284495-2002)

Island Helicopters International: Hop on Island Helicopters International, the only Caribbean helicopter charter operator in the British Virgin Islands, for a scenic, safe, and hassle-free shuttle flight from many Caribbean airports directly to your destination. Island Helicopters International can make BVI travel much smoother and quicker by meeting your party personally at the gate. (284-495-2538)

ACKEE LOWDOWN

Ackee, used in almost every favorite BVI breakfast, often plays a dual role. In all actuality, it is a fruit, but most hometown heroes in the islands treat it as a favorite veggie.

And when dished up it looks, and tastes, like scrambled eggs.

Ackee is a new phenomenon for many, as it's not typically shipped to other parts of the world. A word to the wise: make sure to eat the fruit at the right time of year. In other words, if Ackee is not ripe—it tastes awful and its seeds are even poisonous at certain times of the year.

Add in some salt fish, and you have a mean dish! Salt fish, which is simply cod or mackerel cured in salt, gives ackee the zing that has made it all the rage.

If you don't have the ingredients to make it yourself, keep an eye out around the islands (try the Dog & Dolphin on Virgin Gorda), as many local eateries will serve ackee and salt fish. If not, don't be afraid to ask—you might just get lucky.

ACKEE AND SALT FISH

Ingredients:
2 dozen ackees (in pods) or 1 tin of ackees
1 fresh sprig of thyme
½ lb salt cod fish
1 fresh hot pepper
2 tbsp butter
1 small to medium tomato, chopped
¼ cup oil
2 onions, sliced
Pepper to taste

Locals Do It Like This:
Picking the perfect scarlet ackee pods is the trick—seek out those that are completely open with the black seed and yellow fruit clearly visible. Note: unripe ackees contain a highly toxic substance, so be picky.

Remove the ackees from the pods, discarding the seeds and pink membrane of each fruit. Wash the fruit and then boil it in a large pot of water along with the tasty salt fish. When the ackees are tender, drain the water, and separate the ackees from the fish. Remove the bones and skin from the fish, and then flake.

Heat the butter and oil in a frying pan. Add the onions, thyme, hot pepper, and tomato. Stir together and add the flaked salt fish. Continue to stir lightly while adding the drained ackees. Sprinkle with freshly ground black pepper. Serve with eggs, and consider tossing in some fried plantains or avocado slices.

For a different twist, try ackee pie by lining a pie tin with pastry and fill it with ackee and salt fish. Top heavily with cheese, and bake for 45 minutes at 400°F.

THE ISLANDS BEST FISH FRY

- Any roadside stand in Little Apple Bay, just drive along Tortola's North Beach and look for a grouping of roadside stalls under the big banyan tree near Zion Hill Road. This fish fry is perfect for those staying in the Sugar Mill Hotel who want an easy stroll to sample the island's local treats. Go on a Friday night!

- Quito's Gazebo (284-495-4837) in the North Shore features a mouth watering Wednesday night Fish Fry.

- Though Da Wedding in Cane Garden Bay hasn't offered any late night activity by local fishing legend Poui as of late, this will always be a good spot for eats. Call ahead, if you can catch Poui at lunchtime you'll be treated to a fresh catch.

- Myett's in Cane Garden Bay (284-495-9649) offers an unforgettable fry, at times complete with live music by local bands such as 02B.

- At one time Ceta's Place in Cappoon's Bay, on Tortola, was the only place to be on Thursday nights. The informal gathering, live music, and sizzling fish have ceased for the time being, but keep your fingers crossed that Ceta may one day soon reinvent her gift shop, bringing back the popular fish fry!

- Trellis Bay Village, on the eastern tip of Tortola, is home to Aragorn's Studio and shore side shops packed with local spices and island produce. Aragom, a local legend, is an active farmer who works with a network of local farmers who bring their produce to the "Fruit Depot." Things really heat up during the Trellis Bay Fish Fry or the Full Moon Party that often take place on the beach.

THE ISLAND'S BEST LOCAL GOODIES

- Pam's Kitchen: Located by Neptune's Treasure on Anegada, Pam's is the best source for fine baked goods and homemade jams. Now run by Pam's daughter, Michelle, Pam's Kitchen will even dinghy out to anchored boats to peddle their local kitchen creations. Pam's Kitchen can be reached at 284-495-9439.

- Sailor's Ketch: This is the spot if you're looking for fresh fish (tuna, dolphin, and swordfish) caught by local folks. Plus, Sailor's Ketch will even deliver to your boat. Check them out at www.sailorsketch.com.

- Nature's Basket: Located in Great Harbour on Jost Van Dyke, Nature's Basket offers the freshest locally grown fruits and veggies. Nature's Basket can be reached at 284-495-9312.

- Christine's Bakery: Situated on Jost Van Dyke, Christine's Bakery provides one heck of a breakfast and other local goodies to stock your villa or boat. Christine's can be reached at 284-495-9281.

- Kelly's: This local hangout has been dishing up what many BVIslanders will argue is the best local food for decades.

- Aragorn's Island Produce: Aragom, a local farming phenom, provides a steady supply of island spices, seasonings and herbal bush teas. Particularly noteworthy are Aragom's cinnamon sticks, nutmeg and mace, island coffee, Salt Island salt, cassava cereal, arrowroot, and island chocolate.

- Rose in Carrot Bay: Locals know her, so don't be afraid to ask around. Rose sells the freshest locally grown produce everyday starting at 3pm. When you find her, ask Rose about her vegetarian restaurant (her family grows all of the organic produce).

TORTOLA TIDBIT:

Tortola is home to a colorful mix of culinary options; explore them all! Nestled on a hillside, just past the corner on Main Street, is the Roti Palace (284-494-4196). Try the roti (crepe-like wrap) or any dish that uses the local fruit of choice: breadfruit. Come dinnertime, Mrs. Scatliffe's (284-495-4556) in Carrot Bay can't be topped when her famous Chicken and Coconut recipe is being served. With candlelight and fungi entertainment (music indigenous to the islands), this eatery provides the kind of unique dining experience that many visitors rave about to friends and family back home for years to come.

LOCALLY GROWN

Sure the organic craze sweeping the globe is fine and dandy, but opting for locally grown BVI produce is always your best bet. When you gobble up locally grown BVI goodies, you gain not only better taste, but also better insight into the local community. In the British Virgin Islands much of the organically grown food is imported, and comes with a hefty price tag. As an alternative, locally grown goods can be found in many markets and BVI restaurants. Look around, you're sure to find locally grown fruits, vegetables, and fine herbs that provide the real taste of the islands. Best of all, by eating healthier local foods, you're also getting to know and supporting the people who are taking care of the BVI landscape. When in BVI, look for the local restaurants and supermarkets that support BVI farmers!

ROASTED BREADFRUIT AND SALTFISH

Ingredients:
1 large breadfruit
¼ cup water
1 lb salt fish
1 onion
1 tomato
¼ cup oil
1 small cucumber
1 tsp butter

Locals Do It Like This:
Start by roasting the breadfruit, and slicing it when cooled. Next boil the salt fish. Clean, and break the salt fish into small pieces. Dice the tomatoes and onions, and slice the cucumber. Add to the salt fish. Heat oil in a frying pan and add the salt fish along with the other ingredients and let it simmer. Make sure to serve it hot!

BARBECUED LOBSTER WITH LIME BUTTER

Ingredients:
4 lobsters
1 roasted red bell pepper
2 tablespoon oil
1 cup butter (softened)
2 limes
2 garlic cloves (chopped)
¼ cup fresh chives (chopped)
Fresh ground black pepper

Locals Do It Like This:
Begin by bringing a large pot of salted water to a boil and plunge the lobster into the water for approximately five minutes. Remove and cool. Begin to half the lobster lengthwise and remove the viscera. Next, mix the roasted red pepper with the butter, lime juice, and garlic in a food processor or blender until smooth. Rub the mixture on the lobster and let stand for twenty-five minutes. Once time has elapsed, you're ready to barbecue your tasty lobster (flesh side down) on the grill until it turns a beautiful golden color. Turn the lobster and brush the flesh with the butter sauce and cook for another seven minutes. Top your creation with any remaining butter sauce and serve.

RECOMMENDED READ:

Don't Stop the Carnival by Herman Wouk (Little Brown and Co. 1965) is a favorite Caribbean novel that's not to be missed.

Diving British Virgin Islands by Jim and Ooile Scheiner (AcquaQuest Books 1997) is packed with info, site diagrams, and the photography of one the most well-known BVI photojournalists.

The Sugar Mill Caribbean Cookbook: Casual and Elegant Recipes Inspired by the Islands by Jinx and Jefferson Morgan (Harvard Common Press 1996). Former *Bon Appétit* food and wine critics, Jinx and Jefferson Morgan now operate the famed Sugar Mill Restaurant and have brought their Caribbean cuisine to the masses in one of the best BVI publications to date.

Sky Juice and Flying Fish by Jessica B. Harris (Fireside 1991). One heck of an authentic guide to Caribbean cooking and regional specialties.

Sunfun Calypso, authored by Islander Julian Putley (Virgin Island Books 1999), is an absolute must for any fan of the Caribbean. Packed with laughter, poignancy, and tons of hometown lowdown, *Sunfun Calypso* is the perfect adventure whether you're a tourist, an avid BVI traveler, or resident. Putley, who is to this day a popular yachtsman in the BVI's, has spent many years navigating the Caribbean as a yacht charter captain. Putley also freelances for *BVI Welcome* magazine and publishes other tropical tales. He is a BVI fixture that you'll want to read and, if possible, meet in person. Many lucky travelers will tell tales of Putley serving as their skipper, only to find out later that he's the talent behind quite possibly the best BVI book to date. In fact, after you read his descriptions of island cooking, the sea, and the sun, you'll be ready to hire him to charter your next trip.

Hurricanes and Hangovers is written by Miss Mermaid, the famed island blogger with a top secret identity. This book packs a punch and is brimming with 16 stories of madness and mayhem of life afloat and ashore in the Caribbean. Meet colorful drunks, gamblers, sailors, pirates and prostitutes. While many stories are based on truth, characters and scenes have been disguised to protect the guilty, the famous and the infamous.

Hurricanes and Hangovers, by Miss Mermaid

CALLALOO AND FUNGI

You'll either love it or hate it, but either way, you have to try it! Much like grits, fungi is a cornmeal hodgepodge that some describe as corn-bread while others liken it to grits. Toss in callaloo, which is very similar to spinach, and you have yourself an island favorite. However, the real popularity of the dish is due to the fresh crabs and the very hot pepper sauce that most island cooks secretly toss in to every good dish of callaloo and fungi.

HOW TO MAKE CALLALOO REALLY POP:

Old school BVIslanders will tell you that the only way to make authentic Callaloo is to toss in fried fish, salted pork, and ground provisions. Callaloo is also popular in Guyana, Barbados, Grenada, Haiti, Dominica, Jamaica, and Trinidad & Tobago.

Did You Know?
Dr. Reyes, a Naturopathic Physician and Nutritional Consultant for Nature's Way Ltd., provides consultation services at convenient locations throughout the British Virgin Islands. Schedule an appointment by calling 284-494-6393 or 284 494-6829.

TUNA AND STEAMED CALLALOO

Ingredients:
1 8 oz tuna steak
1 cup seasoned flour
1 cup egg wash
3 cup fry shortening

Dipping Sauce:
1 Scotch bonnet diced small, deseeded
6 oz orange juice reduced by boiling to 3 oz or 50% of the volume
1 garlic clove, diced
3 oz whole lightly salted butter
Steamed Callaloo

Locals Do It Like This:
Use the flour and egg to batter the tuna. Fry in 350° oil until golden brown on the outside. Drain on paper towel.

Next is the sauce: start by adding the Scotch bonnet and garlic to the orange juice. Add butter and whisk until the sauce has just begun to boil. Now steam the callaloo for 4 minutes in lemon juice. Place the steamed callaloo on a plate, with the fish on top. Serve the sauce on the side. A tropical fruit wedge is always a nice touch!

OTHER FAVORITE EATS ...

Flying Fish

These small, silver fish are commonly found on the menu at The Mine Shaft on Virgin Gorda. Their rigid fins, which resemble dragonfly wings, have taken the breath away from sailors for years while propelling themselves through the air at speeds of up to thirty miles per hour.

Grouper Sandwich

Making their home in shallow to mid-range reefs, these sweet, mild-tasting fish are great for lunch. You'll want to drop a line to snag one. When fried in a proper batter and placed on a bun, the fish becomes the centerpiece for almost every Caribbean menu that carries a catch-of-the-day selection. But to appreciate the real beauty of the grouper sandwich, fix one yourself and enjoy it on your boat at midday or on a beachfront picnic table.

Rice and Peas

Also known as "Pigeon Peas," this BVI fave originated in Africa and is now a popular Caribbean side dish (especially at Myett's). Consider adding this side concoction to spicy dishes for a nice balance to hot eats.

West Indian Sauce

The basic recipe for this island standby calls for onion, garlic, and chili peppers sautéed with red and green bell peppers, along with tomatoes and homemade broth (made with fish bones or crustacean shell). Use it on everything!

Christophene

A favorite incredible edible, christophene (also called chocho and chayote) belongs to the gourd family and is a favorite of BVIslanders. Pear-shaped with coarse wrinkles and green skin, inside christophene boast white flesh with a texture that is a cross between a cucumber and a potato. Chef Joe on the *Braveheart*, a fully equipped fifty-four-foot private crewed catamaran, is but one of the many kitchen phenoms in BVI who dazzle guests with christophene. Aboard *Braveheart*, Joe stuffs and bakes his christophene fruit with cheese and breadcrumbs au gratin. And Joe isn't the only one doing christophene right, on Norman Island at Pirates Bight, guests dine on the fruit as a side dish with their roti.

Ground Provisions

Don't be surprised if you hear crops of dasheen, yams, and sweet potatoes simply called "ground provisions" in the islands.

Heat and Eat

Yes, even islanders are tempted by good old-fashioned TV dinners (but with a twist). Ms. Penguin offers the islands a local "heat and eat" gourmet option, proving that convenient can also mean tasty. Those looking to dine on local goodies in the comfort of their own villa or boat can preorder online by contacting Ms. Penguin at www.mspenguin.com.

? JUST ASK A LOCAL:

Think of the Virgin Islands, of sandy beaches and placid waters, and you most likely think of St. Thomas or St. John. However, the British portion of the Virgin Islands shares the same simple pleasures and idyllic lifestyle as well, just with a tad more subtlety.

The British Virgin Islands, within eyeshot of the U.S. Virgin Islands, may lack the hustle and bustle of the mainland, but they make up for it with distinct and hidden gems. You just have to know where to find them.

Peering at the Caribbean on a world map, it's a bit difficult to distinguish between the 50 or so islands and cays that make up the British Virgin Islands. About 90 miles east of Puerto Rico and northeast of the U.S. Virgin Islands, your best bet is to find information the old fashioned way: just ask a local.

Seeking out the wise advice of friendly locals almost always produces hidden treasures, not to mention new friendships. A friendly chat with a cabbie, a store clerk, or someone simply passing by will result in numerous insider tips and anecdotes rich in history and charm.

A local islander on Tortola, for example, would most likely direct you to Palm's Delight, (284) 495-4863, a local haven for family-style West Indian dishes and a killer fish Creole in Carrot Bay -- or perhaps Crandall's Pastry Plus for the best johnnycakes around. Similarly, the friendly locals on Jost Van Dyke will likely send you to Sidney's Peace and Love for Sidney's reef lobster and secret family recipes, all paid on the honor system.

BVI JERK CHICKEN

Ingredients:
1 ½ lb skinless boneless chicken
6 green onions
1 medium onion
2 Scotch bonnet pepper, seeded and minced
¾ cup soy sauce
½ cup red wine vinegar
¼ cup coconut oil
¼ cup brown sugar
2 tbsp fresh thyme leaves
1 tsp cloves, crushed
1 tsp black peppercorns, crushed
1 tsp ground cloves
½ tsp ground nutmeg
½ tsp ground allspice
¼ tsp ground cinnamon

Locals Do It Like This:
Cut the chicken breasts into strips, and set aside in a bowl. Combine all of the other ingredients and mix (or use a food processor). Pour the mixture over the chicken and cover for eight hours or overnight. Remove the chicken and place on a grill, cooking for four to five minutes per side.

THINGS YOU SHOULDN'T MISS:

◇ Don't miss a diving experience with Dive BVI (dbvi@caribsurf.com, or 284-495-5513), as they're the best in all the islands. These folks are also quick to provide dive equipment sales and rentals.

◇ Don't miss a chance to float with the crew at Double D's. Think private charters, specialized attention, and the most knowledgeable of staff. Make sure to ask for Caryn, one of the best in the group, and she'll take you to some of her favorite dive spots, such as "The Indians," and then lunch at Willy T's.

◇ Don't miss the Bath and Turtle Restaurant on Wednesday night. You'll want to catch their "Jump Up," a local treat with live music and freely flowing drinks. Go early for a seat.

◇ Don't miss one of the most romantic and hidden beaches in BVI, Dead Man's Bay, an unbeatable swatch of beach located on Peter Island.

◇ Don't miss a massage on the beach from the posh Little Dix Bay Resort (ldbhotel@surfbvi.com, or 284-495-5555).

◇ Don't miss an opportunity to watch Mocko Jumbies, or Sky Dancers, perched atop heavy wooden stilts. Often entertaining a crowd along Waterfront Drive in Road Town, Mocko Jumbies are a hit with children and adults alike. You can also find Mocko Jumbies at Trellis Bay's Full Moon Parties on Beef Island.

◇ Don't miss parasailing out of Leverick Bay, Virgin Gorda (284-495-7376).

◇ Don't miss a chance to stay, or at least take a stroll, along White Bay on Jost Van Dyke. Boasting a long white sand beach, the area is as popular with sunbathers and beachcombers as it is with boaters who flock to the bay due to its protective reefs. White Bay is also home to the Sandcastle (284-495-9888), a small hideaway resort with a handful of cottages and rooms.

Courtesy of Soggy Dollar Bar

White Bay, Jost Van Dyke

♦ MOBILE BBQ

If you can find it, seek out J Blakx Jerk BBQ, a fine BBQ rig on wheels. Offering some of the best pork on the islands, J Blakx Jerk BBQ is a tasty insider's find. Look for him in Road Town, or call 284-495-1382.

♦ HOW TO WORK OFF THE Q

After feasting on barbeque in the British Virgin Islands you'll most certainly need a way to work off all of the gastronomical fun. One surefire way is by trekking to Chicken Rock, known by many locals as the best hike in the islands. Located on Guana Island (15-minute boat ride from Trellis Bay Marina), Chicken Rock is part of the 850-acre island where 65 percent is left untouched. With flora and fauna galore, a hike to Chicken Rock, on the northwest point, takes you through empty beaches, orchids, and a few harmless snakes. The rock, which actually looks just like a chicken, can be reached in approximately one hour. Those lucky few who know about Chicken Rock are rewarded with not only an unbeatable hike, but also a deep blue pool below its base.

 PORK CHOPS WITH BACON AND BANANA

Ingredients:
4 pork chops
¾ tsp cumin
Juice of one lemon
2 tbsp butter
2 bananas
6 strips of bacon
1 Carib beer
Salt and pepper

Locals Do It Like This:
Melt the butter and add the salt, pepper, and cumin to create a rub and work it into both sides of the pork chop. Next, peel the bananas and slice into 1 ¼ inch pieces. Situate the bananas on a dish and top with freshly squeezed lemon juice. Wrap each piece of banana with a slice of bacon and place on skewers (threading where the bacon overlaps) and set aside. Grill the pork chops for approximately 15 minutes, turning only once. Lowering the heat, add the bananas wrapped in bacon and grill for an additional 10 minutes, again turning the meat as well as the bananas. While the meat is cooking, use one bottle of Carib beer to baste the meat.

MORE THINGS YOU SHOULDN'T MISS

◇ Don't miss the thrill of riding along the tiny road (watch out for the goats) going over Gorda Peak. With its airplane-like vantage point, you'll get a view of all the nearby islands. Take your camera.

◇ Don't miss callaloo—a well-seasoned West Indian soup that contains fresh ingredients such as okra, chili peppers, and sometimes crab.

◇ Don't miss a plane ride with Warren, owner of Caribbean Wings. Warren is a retired airline pilot who now runs a private charter business, shuttling wide-eyed tourists to and from Virgin Gorda's tiny landing strip. With a bird's-eye view of the island, Warren will point out sugar mill ruins, rock formations, and a number of excellent flats for bonefishing just before an always smooth landing.

◇ Don't miss an opportunity to gawk at Roseate Flamingos, the beautiful shorebird found near the salt ponds on the western half of Anegada.

◇ Don't miss a chance to try your hand at the best windsurfing in BVI—seek out Pomato Point or Setting Point. For another option, give Cane Garden Bay—inside its reef—a chance as well.

◇ Don't miss the BVI Grand Festival Parade in Road Town. Music and dance, along with endless supplies of local food and drink, make this lively festival the perfect time to delve into island culture. The BVI Grand Festival Parade is held on August Monday, (first Monday).

◇ Find more "Don't Miss" tips at www.islandlowdown.com

◇ Don't miss tasting an authentic Painkiller at the Soggy Dollar Bar, the birthplace of BVI's most famous tropical concoction.

Courtesy of Soggy Dollar Bar

A bartender at the Soggy Dollar Bar serves the world famous Painkiller.

☞ BLAFF

When dropped into boiling water what sound do you hear? Blaff. Or at least that's what locals say. Known as poached fish in many parts of the world, islanders simply call it Blaff.

Many swear by red snapper marinated with allspice, garlic, Scotch bonnet chili, and lime juice. When onion, thyme, chives, and parsley are added to water, locals drop the red snapper into the boiling water for the best "blaff" in town.

Traditionalists serve the fish with some liquid in a bowl. It's also very common to see island chefs add a splash of white wine, referring to it as their spiced version. Either way, blaff is a good way to avoid using your boat's oven!

◉ OKRA

Okra is often fried and served as a popular side dish in BVI. Okra is often combined with cornmeal to make one heck of a local dish, known as fungi and served with seafood.

BLAFF

Ingredients:
6 allspice berries, crushed
3 cloves garlic, crushed
1 Scotch bonnet chili
6 limes, juiced
1 ½ qt water
1 small onion, sliced
1 sprig fresh thyme
1 sprig parsley
4 small red snappers, scaled and cleaned, but keep the heads intact
Salt and freshly ground pepper to taste

Locals Do It Like This:
Prepare the marinade by cutting the allspice in half, then add half the lime juice, one garlic clove, chili, salt, and fresh pepper. Pour the mixture over the red snapper in a bowl and marinade for a minimum of two hours.

When ready to cook, place remaining ingredients (with the exception of the other half of lime juice) in a heavy pot and bring to a heavy boil. When the water is boiling at its peak, plop the fish into it and listen for the "blaff!" Allow the water to return to a boil and then remove the fish.

Locals serve blaff in bowls covered with any remaining marinade and lime juice. Blaff is best served with white rice.

COLAS DE RES (OXTAIL)

Serves 4

Ingredients:
6 lbs oxtail
2 lbs tomatoes
1 lb onion
1 tbsp local salt
1 head garlic

Locals Do It Like This:
Begin by chopping the onions and tomatoes. Mince the garlic. Next, place the oxtail in a pot of water and add the onion, tomatoes, and garlic. Bring to a boil. Finally, lower the heat and keep it on low for approximately 4 hours. Cook until tender.

BBQ MACKEREL

Ingredients:
1 large whole mackerel
Juice of 3 limes
10 cm piece of ginger (finely chopped)
2 Scotch bonnets (deseeded and finely chopped)
3 garlic cloves (finely chopped)
2 bunches of green onions (finely chopped)
Fresh thyme sprigs
Salt
Fresh ground black pepper

Locals Do It Like This:
Rub the mackerel with the lime juice and all seasonings, and marinate for a minimum of two hours. When ready, grill your tasty mackerel creation until the fish flakes, or wrap it in foil and bake for forty minutes.

☞ LOOK FOR GLORIA!

For some of the best oxtail around, pop into Midtown Restaurant located on Main and Chalweel Streets in Tortola. Gloria, the owner of this fine local establishment, will prepare an unforgettable meal for you, capped off with her famous peanut punch and mauby.

🧀 TRY SOME SOUSE

Not always the first on most tourists' list, Souse (also known as brawn, head cheese or pig's trotters) is a traditional local dish that can be found at fairs, festivals, and many hidden gems such as Midtown Restaurant. Give it a try; you'll be surprised.

🎤 ASK FOR HENNY:

On Anegada, a hometown hero known simply as "Henny" will show you the way. Just ask around, and locals will point you to her goodies that often find their way to local markets. If you can manage some face-time with this charming islander, snag it, you won't be disappointed. From a small garden behind her stucco house, Henny will let you sample ripe tomatoes, eggplant, peppers, and callaloo. She also has a small herd of goats. Best of all -- Henny keeps things organic and bypasses all chemicals. If you chat long enough you'll learn that this popular islander is also known for the very best sea grape jelly in quite possibly the entire world.

⚓ TAMARIND TIDBIT

Though much of the subtropical forest was cleared for sugar cane production in the 1700s, there is now a strong outcropping of wild tamarind, mango trees, hibiscus, frangipani, and cacti on the hillsides. Look for mangroves and palms along the shoreline.

🍴 OTHER CARIBBEAN BBQ TIDBITS:

If you love the 'cue, then head over to the colorful Sidney's Peace and Love Restaurant (284-494-4941) on Jost Van Dyke in Little Harbour (284-495-9271). Sure the lobster dinners are all the rage, but don't pass up a chance to sample some of the best BBQ ribs in BVI. BBQ loyalists will also want to try C&F Restaurant (284-494-4941) on Tortola for some super fine BBQ.

🏆 DIG THE PIG:

Bryan Hodge, of Tortola, operates one of the best BVI hog farms and supplies the territory's top restaurants with grade-A pork. Winner of the "BVI Best Pig Farmer" honor by the Government's Agriculture Department, Hodge (along with his son, brother, and nephew) is considered a hometown hero for his livestock farming techniques. This family operation uses Duroc, Yorkshire, and Lanrae breed of pigs to ensure the finest quality of meat. Best of all, Hodge's pigs are given only naturally grown feed. Many pig roasts held by Bitter End Yacht Club, Norman Island, and Necker Island rely only on Hodge's quality product.

TAMARIND BARBECUE LAMB

Ingredients:
4 large lamb chops
2 cups tamarind syrup
1 onion, diced
4 tbsp garlic, chopped
2 cups white vinegar
½ cups brown sugar
2 cups ketchup
5 bay leaves
2 large cassava
1 onion, julienned
2 green peppers, julienned
2 garlic cloves, minced
2 cup coconut oil
1 cup white vinegar
1 cup cilantro, chopped
Salt and pepper
Fresh parsley
2 limes, juiced
Scotch Bonnet for seasoning (optional)
Avocado slices for garnish

Locals Do It Like This:
Begin with the tasty sauce: sauté the garlic and onions; and then add the syrup, vinegar, brown sugar, ketchup, and bay leaves. Reduce to a thick syrup. Next, cover the lamb in the sauce and then sear it. Remove from heat and then bake at 350° for 8 to 10 minutes. Meanwhile, sauté the onions, cassava, peppers, and garlic in coconut oil. Cover and season with salt, pepper, lime, and Scotch bonnet sauce (optional). Garnish with fresh avocado and parsley.

CARIBBEAN CHILI

Ingredients:
5 lbs ground sirloin
2 lbs sweet Italian sausage
3 onions, chopped
2 green bell peppers, chopped
2 sweet red bell peppers, chopped
2 fresh green roasted Scotch bonnet peppers, seeded and minced
4 garlic cloves, minced
⅓ cup chili powder
1 tbsp sea salt
2 tsp dried oregano
2 tsp ground cumin
2 bay leaves
1 oz dried cilantro leaf
3 cans (28 oz) whole tomatoes, undrained
½ cup yellow cornmeal
2 cans (16 oz) pink beans, drained
2 cans (16 oz) black beans, drained
Scallions

Locals Do It Like This:
Pull out your largest kettle for this winning tropical recipe. Begin by removing the sausage from its casing and add it to the kettle. Add the onions, red and green peppers, Scotch bonnet chili peppers, and garlic. Cook over medium-high heat. Make sure to stir often for approximately 10 minutes. Drain excess fat and add chili powder, oregano, salt, cumin, bay leaves, and cilantro. Stir for an additional minute. Next, add the tomatoes with their puree and bring to a boil. Reduce the heat to low and simmer for approximately 1½ hours (until the liquid is reduced). In a small bowl to the side, mix the cornmeal and ½ cup of water. Stir this cornmeal mixture—as well as the pink and black beans—into the chili. Continue to cook for ten minutes until the chili is thick. Top with scallions, and serve with Johnny Cake. Be prepared, the Scotch bonnet makes this one especially hot!

CHILI COOK-OFF

If you're island hopping in July, check out the Firecracker 500 Regatta & Chili Cook-off!

GUINNESS MARINATED BABY BACK RIBS:

Hodges Creek Marina, in Maya Cove, is home to Fat Hog Bob's, every yachtsman's favorite spot for baby back ribs. Fat Hog Bob steps it up a notch and marinates their version in a secret chef's sauce made of Guinness. Hog size portions can be enjoyed on a one hundred-foot covered porch. (284-495-1010)

MELON AND PROSCIUTTO:

Need an easy hors d'oeuvre idea for a dinner under the stars on your boat or villa? Then try wrapping cantaloupe wedges in prosciutto and secure with toothpicks. Add a dash of Sherry Pepper Sauce on each.

DOWN THE SHADY HIKING TRAIL

Down the shady hiking trail toward the entrance to The Baths, wide-eyed first-time visitors imagine the sorts of tropical fish and treasures they'll find among the famed boulders along Virgin Gorda's shores. While the outcropping of house-size rocks and lagoons are spectacular, and the panoramic views truly breath-taking, locals know that this is merely a tourist "thang." The real appeal of the British Virgin Islands is found much deeper inland, out of reach of the typical day tripper or sailor just happening by.

Just ask Edith, the bartender at Mad Dog's, perched on the rocks just above The Baths. Known locally, and perhaps even worldwide, as the creator of the best piña colada. With her quiet and unassuming way, she'll politely decline questions related to her secret cocktail ingredients but will happily point you to the best kept secrets on the island (she's quite the dancer and knows the local hot spots).

Take for instance, the Mine Shaft Full Moon Party, held each month down a winding road on this 10-mile-long tropical paradise. Lincoln, also called "All Out," and his brother Jinx are jovial fixtures at the restaurant and are always sure to fill you in on the local "sip-sip" (gossip). You're likely to be offered the brothers' famous "Cave In," a mighty concoction that is kept top secret. Be prepared – Lincoln will happily plop a miner's helmet on your head and lower a bucket of various types of liquor from the ceiling in celebration of patrons brave enough to attempt the beverage.

From atop the Mine Shaft's large hillside deck, guests are treated to island music, new friends, and excellent local dishes like roti, Anegada grouper, and stewed conch with local spices.

Straying even farther from the beaten path, but still only footsteps away from anchoring cruise ships, you'll find ideal spots for beachcombing, local restaurant hopping, and game fishing — tarpon, barracuda, bone fish, and jacks. The most adventurous travelers will take the locals' suggestion to take island exploring even further by heading down to Yacht Harbor to seek out an island guide who can show you the lay of the land by car or boat. Sanford Harringan is a solid pick for transportation (he has a taxi and boat) – just look for a man at the Bath & Turtle's outside bar with a bright yellow shirt, a walkie-talkie, and a huge smile.

Chatting with locals in the area, especially around the docks, will lead to the advice to go island-hopping to neighboring hot spots like Ginger, Cooper, Salt, Peter, and Norman. If you can find someone to take you even farther, try to snag a boat ride over to Anegada, known as the "Sunken Island." There you'll be treated to the most elemental aspects of island life: primeval seclusion with miles and miles of untouched beach. If you can manage to make it this far your reward will be the local Anegada lobster and a story shared with only a lucky few.

After a safe return to Virgin Gorda on your boat, you'll be happy that you spent time exploring the many untouched aspects of island life. The piña colada at Mad Dog's will taste that much better when you tell all the other tourists that you ventured far beyond the glossy postcard version of The Baths.

◇ Mad Dog's, (284) 495-5830, open 10am to 7pm daily.

◇ Toad Hall (284) 495-5397, located just below Mad Dog, is the perfect spot to keep an eye on The Baths, but from your own private series of villas built literally between the boulders.

◇ The Mine Shaft (284) 495-5260, www.mineshaftbvi.com.

◇ The Spirit of Anegada (284) 496-6825, a 44-foot gaff-rigged schooner, captained by Keith Williams, offering day sails and private charters to Anegada.

◇ Sanford Harrigan Taxi (284) 543-3984/VHF Ch #16, is a reliable – and enjoyable – ride guide.

◇ Little Dix Bay (284) 495-5555, an all-inclusive resort, offers 98 suites on Virgin Gorda, ranging from four to six thousand dollars for the week.

ISLAND ESCAPADES

BVI consists of more than sixty islands, cays, and rocks. Though a complete list is hard to come by, it's advisable to dig up every map and nautical chart possible and explore them all. A sample of a few of the best includes:

Guana Island: A tranquil 850-acre island that was once a sugar cane plantation, now a private resort.

Buck Island: A tiny uninhabited island that offers excellent snorkeling along the north coast.

Scrub Island: A 230-acre private tropical paradise with lush foliage, it is one mile from Tortola.

Sandy Spit: A picture-perfect deserted island, it is the kind you dream about. A popular day anchorage.

The Dogs: Six small, uninhabited islands that are home to some of the best scuba diving and snorkeling.

Fallen Jerusalem: Just off the tip of Virgin Gorda, Fallen Jerusalem is uninhabited and rocky, yet home to a tiny beach worth visiting.

Great Camanoe: An uninhabited island that has a vibrant reef for snorkeling. There are moorings in Cam Bay.

Little Camanoe: Also uninhabited, Little Camanoe offers a popular diving spot just off the northeast tip.

Ginger Island: An uninhabited island made popular by Alice in Wonderland, this is a diving destination.

Little Thatch: A private fifty-four-acre island that is home to the Sea Grape Cottage.

Jost Van Dyke: The smallest of the four main islands of BVI, it is named after a Dutch privateer.

Marina Cay: A family-friendly island, it is complete with Pusser's restaurant and Robb White Bar. There is a free ferry from Trellis Bay.

Dead Chest: An uninhabited national park that serves as a popular diving destination (Coral Gardens, Dead Chest West, and Painted Walls).

Eustatia Island: A tiny private island that has a handful of villas.

The Indians: An excellent diving and snorkeling spot, the Indians are made up of four pinnacles worth exploring. Several moorings are available.

Saba Rock: A tiny island boasting a restaurant, bar, gift shop, and small resort.

The Tobagos: Rugged cliffs and cays make up this BVI National Park. It is perfect for both bird watching and diving. Check out Mercurious Rock.

Moskito Island: A 125-acre oasis that is complete with popular snorkeling spots at Honeymoon Beach and Anguilla Point.

◆ BAKED CHICKEN AND A VIEW

Try the Top of the Baths Restaurant (284-495-5497) not only for a tasty chicken entrée but also for a striking panoramic view! If you don't like your chicken baked, they offer many varieties including a mean jerk chicken dish.

◆ POULTRY FARMERS:

Khoy Smith, an up-and-coming businessman in the BVI's, owns Prophies Farm. As the conduit between other poultry farmers and local supermarkets, Smith assists his fellow chicken enthusiasts with processing and selling their chickens throughout the territory.

Other Fine Farmers:

Ask anyone about the best, and "Aukie" is sure to be referenced. Renardis "Aukie" Donovan-Fahie is directly responsible for the bulk of fruits and vegetables in the best restaurants and markets throughout the British Virgin Islands. Meanwhile, out on the water, BVIslanders (and tourists) have Kevin Grey, a top commercial fisherman, to thank for supplying the area with the best lobster.

 BAKED CHICKEN AND GUAVA SAUCE

Ingredients:
3 ¼ lbs. chicken, cut into 6 to 8 serving pieces
1 stalk scallion, chopped
½ onion, chopped
2 cloves garlic, chopped
1 tbsp vegetable oil
3 ¼ lbs. chicken, cut into 6 to 8 serving pieces
1½ guava pulp, chopped
1 cup guava juice
½ tomato ketchup
¼ whole ginger
1 tbsp brown sugar
4 cups water
¼ white cane vinegar
Fresh black pepper to taste

Locals Do It Like This:
Begin by chopping the scallion, garlic, and onion, then blend ingredients together with the vegetable oil. Next, season the chicken with the blend and marinate it for at least one hour. Bake the marinated chicken for 40 minutes at 350°F. Meanwhile, make the guava sauce by combining the guava pulp and the guava juice along with ketchup, ginger, sugar, water, and vinegar. Boil together for 15 minutes. Remove the chicken from the oven and spoon the sauce over the chicken. Bake the chicken for an additional 10 minutes with the sauce and remove from heat. Islanders often serve this tasty dish with rice and peas, along with buttered carrots!

TRY SOME BVI BREADFRUIT:

Char-Roasted Breadfruit
Bury a 3 lb breadfruit in the embers of local BVI charcoal for one hour (or on a gas grill). Remove from heat when the breadfruit is soft, and slightly charred. Cut the breadfruit into wedges and serve with butter, salt, and pepper.

Mashed Breadfruit
Remove the top of a 4 lb breadfruit and scoop out the insides. Mix the inside of the breadfruit with coconut cream and butter and stuff back inside. Wrap the breadfruit in foil and grill until tender.

GET TO KNOW BVI FARMERS:

A Handful of the Top Farmers in BVI
Benjamin Peters on Tortola
Lester Maduro on Virgin Gorda
Vera Wheatley on Anegada
Lionel Blyden on Jost Van Dyke

Some of the Best Livestock Farmers
Dr. Clinton George on Tortola
Lester Maduro on Anegada

Best Crop Farmers
Elmore George on Virgin Gorda
Sylvanita Faulkner on Anegada
Eldred Graham on Jost Van Dyke

Best Poultry Farmers
Dr. Clinton George on Tortola
Vera Wheatley on Anegada

Best Orchard Farmers
Michael Loyd on Tortola
Rose Gardener on Virgin Gorda
George Smith on Anegada
Ivan Chinnery on Jost Van Dyke

Best Backyard Gardens
Dr. Brewley on Tortola
Alred Frett on Tortola
Richard Walters on Virgin Gorda
Vera Wheatley on Anegada
Joyce Chinnery on Jost Van Dyke

Other Notable Farmers
Arona George-Dewindt: okra, pineapples, sweet peppers, mangoes, and guava, to name a few.
Stanley Nibbs: bananas, tanya, cabbage, beets, lettuce, and sugar cane.
Silvia Wattley: purple cabbage, ginger, bananas, thyme, celery, parsley, okra, peanuts, and peas.

♦ LOOK FOR JEAN AT ROTI
PALACE

Jean makes some of the best mango chutney on the planet! Think you've had mango chutney before? Think again. Until you've sampled Jean's version, life is just incomplete. Roti Palace (284-494-4196) is located just before The Corner on Main Street on Tortola.

♦ LOOK FOR MOVIENE TOO:

Moviene Fahie, a spirited local businesswoman, is widely known for her farming prowess. Tending to her crops on 2½ acres of farmland at Paraquita Bay, she has won the Woman Farmer of the Year for two years running. Moviene is also known to pass her farming knowledge and love of the land to local children.

BILL'S CARIBBEAN PORK LOIN WITH
MANGO CHUTNEY

Ingredients:
Boneless pork tenderloin
⅓ cup peanut oil
2 tbsp Sunny Caribbee Pepper Blend
1 tsp Kosher salt
4 large mangoes
½ tbsp salt
1 Scotch bonnet
1 ½ cups vinegar
3 garlic cloves, minced
¼ cup gingerroot, chopped
½ cup sugar
¾ seedless raisins

Bill Does It Like This:
Begin with the chutney, peeling and slicing the mangoes and placing them in a bowl with the Scotch bonnet (after removing the seeds), vinegar garlic, gingerroot, and sugar. Bring to a boil, reduce heat, and simmer for 15 minutes (adding mangoes and raisins at the end). Cover and set aside.

Next, rub the pork tenderloin with peanut oil, and season with salt and pepper. Grill the pork loin until tender. Serve with a side of peas and rice, and a healthy dose of mango chutney on the side.

Courtesy of Bill Hartzman & Di Rumsey, Augusta, GA

 LOBSTER PANCAKES

Ingredients:
1 lb sweet potatoes
2 tbsp butter
½ cup milk
1 tsp baking powder
½ cup all-purpose flour
½ tsp nutmeg, freshly grated
Salt and freshly ground black pepper to taste
2 10 oz lobster tails

Garnish (optional):
1 red onion, sliced
¼ cup lobster roe
4 sprigs thyme, or 8 sprigs thyme

Locals Do It Like This:
Start by making the sauce; combine all of the ingredients (except the heavy cream) in a saucepan. Bring to a simmer, and continue to cook for 15 minutes. When the sauce is reduced by two-thirds, begin stirring in the cream. Simmer for an additional 15 minutes and then strain.

Next, begin cooking the lobster. Use salted water to boil the lobster tails for five minutes. Remove the tails (be careful, they'll be hot) and lightly crush each tail. Be sure to remove the meat all in one piece and slice into thin medallions.

Setting aside the lobster tail, start preparing the pancakes. Place butter, salt, and pepper on each sweet potato and wrap individually. Roast the sweet potatoes for an hour at 350° F. Let them cool and begin to mash them in a mixing bowl. Next, mix together the potatoes, eggs, and milk into bowl or food processor. After 10 seconds of mashing, add the baking powder, flour, and nutmeg until the batter is thick and smooth. Now, heat coconut oil in a skillet over medium heat. Dab individual scoops of batter in 3 inch circles in the pan. Watch the batter carefully, when it begins to bubble it's time to add the lobster slice on top before carefully turning the pancakes. Once flipped, cook the pancakes for an additional minute or two. Repeat this process with the remaining batter.

Before serving garnish with sauce, add diced tomatoes, warm grilled onions, and a fresh sprig of thyme for effect. Some islanders add lobster roe too!

LOBSTER PANCAKE SAUCE

Ingredients:
1 cup dry white wine
1 tbsp fresh lemon juice
¼ cup tarragon vinegar
4 shallots, minced
½ tsp peppercorns
1 pint heavy (whipping) cream
2 sprigs parsley

Locals Do It Like This:
In a sauté pan reduce white wine and shallots until nearly dry. Add cream and reduce to a thick consistency, whisking continuously on medium heat. Do not bring to a boil. Add juices and season with salt and pepper.

☞ WHELK

Think escargot and you're very close to what locals call whelk. Technically the West Indian top snail, hometown cooks will tell you that the only way to serve whelk is when it is steamed in sea water and served with a hefty dose of garlic butter. The only exception to the rule? Toss fresh whelk in a roti, just like they do at Roti Palace on Tortola.

▬ HOW TO MAKE FISH
     SAUCE:

Try your hand at this easy recipe. Simply mix bottled clam juice, cut in half with water, simmer with dry white wine, add chopped onion, mushroom trimmings, a drop of lemon juice, pinch of parsley, and reduce in half.

 GRILLED WHELK IN GARLIC BUTTER

Ingredients:
2 dozen small whelk
3 cloves garlic, minced
2 tbsp West Indian chives, minced
1 stick butter, unsalted
Parsley

Locals Do It Like This:
Begin by making the garlic sauce; sauté the minced garlic, butter, jerk seasonings, parsley, and chives until the butter is fully melted and the sauce is clear. Set the sauce aside and grill the whelk, making sure the top side is up. Remove the whelk from its shell and dip it in the garlic sauce. Garnish with a fresh sprig of parsley.

 RUM SCAMPI

Ingredients:
20 jumbo shrimp
2 red bell peppers
½ cup local rum
2 onions, cut in thin slices
4 large garlic cloves
4 tomatoes, small wedges
¾ cup dry white wine
½ cup basic fish sauce
4 tablespoons olive oil
4 tablespoons fresh parsley and chervil, chopped

Locals Do It Like This:
Preheat oven to 375°F and bake red bell peppers for 15 minutes. Let cool and remove skin, seeds, and stems. Chop and set aside. Meanwhile, shell the shrimp and place in a frying pan. Heat four tablespoons of olive oil and cook for two minutes, gently turning shrimp. Pour in the local rum and flame. Move shrimp in the sauce for five to 10 seconds and remove from heat. Add to the pan the pepper, garlic, half of the parsley, half of the chervil, and one tablespoon of olive oil. Let simmer for one minute and then add tomatoes and wine. Stir and simmer for an additional five minutes until the sauce turns light brown. Add the fish sauce and let simmer for eight to 10 minutes. Add salt, pepper, chervil and parsley to taste.

CARIBBEAN GINGER TURKEY

Ingredients:
2 lbs. turkey breast
¼ cup dry sherry
¼ cup soy sauce
2 tbsp apricot jam
½ tsp ginger
½ cup water
¼ cup brown sugar
2 tbsp coconut oil
2 tsp fresh lemon juice
1 clove garlic

Locals Do It Like This:
Carefully debone the turkey breast and remove the skin. Detach the fillet from the underside of the breast by locating the boneless meat beside the breast bone. Cut the breast meat into 4 equal portions. In a bowl combine soy sauce, sugar, dry sherry, oil, apricot jam, lemon juice, ginger, chopped garlic, and water. Mix well. Add the turkey and submerge it in the marinade for at least six hours, preferably overnight. Remove the meat from the marinade and barbecue the turkey for 10 to 15 minutes, turning and brushing with remaining marinade while cooking. Locals serve this dish with rice and a hefty chunk of fruit.

Beach front dining doesn't get any better than on Anegada.

TURKEY DINNER AT JOLLY ROGER INN

Every year the fine folks at Jolly Roger (284-495-4559) on Tortola host a free pot-luck Thanksgiving Dinner. Close to twenty turkeys are cooked each year, and the island regulars bring along all the fixin's!

DON'T FORGET ABOUT THE SIDES:

Island chefs know the secret to any good home-style dish rests in the ability to decorate the plate with the best side items in town. Suggested sides include peas and rice, peas and onions (slice onions in thin strips and sauté in butter before adding to peas and seasoning), garlic carrots, macaroni with tomato sauce, and curried fruit.

☞ TRADITIONAL TIP:

Skillet frying is almost always the best method for home or boat cooking when an adequate deep fryer is not available. When in doubt, locals insist that the best way to go is to simply rub your fish steak with lime juice, score 'em and season 'em, and then dredge the fish in a milk and egg mixture before covering with bread crumbs and frying until golden brown.

☞ TRENDSETTER TIP:

Some more ambitious cooks will abandon the bread crumb route and opt for grated cassava or cooked black beans, both of which can serve as an interesting twist to traditional breading.

TROPICAL BANANA BATTERED SNAPPER

Ingredients:
4-5 filets of snapper
½ cup mashed banana
2 cups of Carib beer
Lemon juice
Salt to taste
2 eggs
½ cup flour
Oil to fry

Locals Do It Like This:
Cut the snapper into small pieces. Soak the fish in water with lemon juice and salt. Meanwhile, mix the banana, eggs, flour, and, of course, add beer to make the tasty batter. Drain the snapper and dip into the batter and fry until golden brown.

The Baths, Virgin Gorda

GOING BANANAS

One of the best traditional cooking ingredients around, the tropical banana leaf is perfect for baking any of the plentiful variety of local fish. Hunting down the banana leaf itself is almost as much fun as cooking with the ornate leaves.

Islanders and adventurous travelers know to seek out the massive banana tree in the valleys and along the mountainsides throughout the islands. Succulent bananas can be found by the handful (five to twenty-five fruits) on the annual banana plant that dies after a glorious nine-month stint.

Removing and searing the banana leaves over a flame until limp, many islanders enjoy dividing the banana leaves into rectangular shapes to fold their fish into neat packages tied with grass strands. Restaurants will often use foil or parchment paper, but you're in the islands; seek out an ornate banana leaf for a creative treat.

You'll want to score some freshly chopped tomatoes and scallions to top off this banana leaf creation. And don't forget the coconut cream; a tropical must! Pop this puppy in the oven for five minutes per one-half inch of thickness at 450° and you'll have yourself an unforgettable and authentic island delicacy in no time.

Throughout the islands you'll most likely hear references to the Sugar Mill Restaurant on Tortola and its variation of fish baked in banana leaves, as well as a variety of recipes that toss in a twist by using lemon, garlic, and ginger. Owners of the Sugar Mill, Jinx and Jefferson Morgan, also treat their guests to everything from banana daiquiri libations to tempting dishes such as fish with tomato and banana. The dynamic duo even offers a killer black-bottom banana pie recipe in their popular read, *The Caribbean Cookbook*.

On Necker Island, Chef Scott Williams serves up an unbeatable banana pudding, drizzled with crème anglaise around the plate. And on Tortola, bananas are so popular that you'll even find villas for rent adorned with names such as "Bananas on the Beach" (284-495-4318).

The Department of Agriculture realizes how bananas BVIslanders are over their bananas and has provided Banana Farmers' Meetings to discuss farming techniques, and how to avoid Moko disease that has hit the plantain and banana sector hard in other countries.

Still need your banana fix? Then try this BVI banana bread recipe on for size:

 BVI BANANA BREAD

Ingredients:
2 large ripe bananas
¾ cup pecan halves
¼ cup raisins
2 cups all-purpose flour
1 tablespoon baking powder
¼ teaspoon fresh nutmeg (grated)
½ teaspoon salt
8 tablespoons butter (softened)
1 teaspoon vanilla extract
½ cup sugar
1 egg
2 teaspoons Pusser's rum

Locals Do It Like This:
Preheat oven to 350°. Chop the pecan halves and add to the raisins and one tablespoon of flour in a bowl. Set aside. Meanwhile, combine baking powder, nutmeg, and salt with the remaining flour. Set aside. Begin peeling the bananas and mash in a bowl, then set aside. Next, cream the butter and sugar together until it is light and fluffy in a large bowl. Add the egg, rum, and bananas, and then stir in the pecan and raisin mixture. Combine with the remaining flour mixture. Place the banana bread batter into a greased loaf pan and bake for fifty minutes.

FISH ESCABECHE

Traditional fish escabeche, also known as escovitch, is prepared with a highly seasoned marinade that is used to preserve this memorable dish. First, your favorite fish is fried and lovingly placed in a large dish. A marinade often made of a heavy dose of lime juice, vinegar, allspice, onions, and Scotch bonnet is then poured on the fish after it has been cooked (while still hot). The entire creation then sits overnight, and is served cold the next day.

Tip: Though this method of cooking can be used for keeping fish for a length of time, it's commonly eaten immediately.

SALMON IN MANGO ESCABECHE

Ingredients:
1 lb cooked salmon
4 cloves garlic
¼ cup vegetable oil
¼ cup olive oil
¼ cup red wine vinegar
¼ cup fresh lime juice
¼ cup chopped ripe, sweet mango
Salt to taste
Coarsely ground black pepper to taste
2 seeded minced jalapeno chilis
1 red onion, peeled and thinly sliced
1 red bell pepper, thinly sliced

Locals Do It Like This:
Start with the escabeche; always start with the escabeche! Begin by chopping the garlic and add the oils, vinegar, lime juice, mango, and salt. Puree until smooth. Next move to the salmon. Once the salmon is cooked you'll want to break it up into large chunks and place it in a baking dish with the red onion and red bell pepper. Now start mixing gently (use your hands to really get into this dish). Cover the dish and refrigerate. Stir the ingredients every 2 hours. In about 6 hours, your escabeche will be ready to eat.

Locals like to serve this dish with cabbage, radishes, jicama, or some form of mixed greens, with the fish and mixture spooned on the top. A chunk of local bread on the side adds a nice finishing touch.

AVOCADO AND MARINATED SHRIMP

Ingredients:
1 lb shrimp
½ tsp fresh lemon juice
2 tbsp white cane vinegar
1 tsp BVI salt
½ tsp mustard powder
1 tsp Scotch bonnet sauce, or hot pepper sauce
3 avocados
6 lettuce or spinach leaves

Locals Do It Like This:
Toss together lemon juice, vinegar, salt, hot pepper sauce, and mustard. Add the shrimp and chill for three hours. Before serving, peel and cut the avocados in half, then brush the halves with the marinade. Arrange the shrimp inside the avocado halves on the bed of lettuce. Serve with any remaining marinade.

♪ LISTEN UP

The popping sounds filling the ears of snorkelers and scuba divers on the reefs are produced by the numerous shrimp populating the BVI's. The two families of shrimp most likely to be seen in the area are Penaeidae and Sicyonidae.

★ SCORE SOME SHRIMP HERE

Pink salmon and shrimp canapés served beachside at the Sugar Mill Resort. (284-495-4355)

Lisa Potter offers a killer shrimp scampi at Potters by the Sea. (284499-9637)

BBQ shrimp at Anegada Reef Hotel (284-495-8002) is not to be missed.

The Soars family, owners of Neptune's Treasure (284-495-9439), offers both a superb stuffed shrimp and sautéed shrimp.

Cow Wreck Beach Bar (284-495-8047) does shrimp right!

Soggy Dollar Bar (284-495-9888) provides a scrumptious shrimp salad wrap.

Pusser's Landing (284-495-4554) is brave enough to offer all-you-can-eat shrimp on Tuesdays (along with an excellent pig roast on Fridays).

Village Cay Restaurant and Bar (284-494-2771) dishes up crab stuffed shrimp, as well as a popular curried shrimp.

THE VOTES ARE IN: BEST PLACES FOR LOCAL FISH

The following use the freshest fish, caught daily at Anegada's North Drop:

- Try the Swordfish at C&F (284-494-4941). Husband and wife super duo, Clarence and Florence pack the house due to the rock bottom prices and freshness of product. For West Indian dishes, you can't beat it.

- Try the Spearfish at Neptune's Treasure (284-495-9439). Ask for Linda, if you're really nice you may squeak out a family recipe or two. Her style, based on a family tradition, is known throughout the islands for its simple, effective approach. Serving her secrets at a tiny bar on the water's edge, you'll be surprised at how far her butter sauce and island spices can go!

- Try the Wahoo at Brandywine Bay (284-495-2301). Chef Davide Pugliese has become a legend because of his Florentine cuisine tucked away in a tiny family inn. You'll want to take your eyes off the excellent view of the Sir Francis Drake Channel in time to eat. And make sure to save some time to talk to Chef Pugliese, as he enjoys personally introducing his unique blend of Caribbean and Tuscan creations. Though the menu changes nightly, try to convince him to make the Wahoo!

- Try the fresh catch of the day offered at Rudy's Bar on Jost Van Dyke. (284-495-9282)

- Try any of the local fish found at the Crab Hole (284-495-5307), a homey eatery in the South Valley on Virgin Gorda.

- Try the wide array of local seafood, caught that day, at Sidney's Peace and Love (284-495-9271) on Jost Van Dyke.

- Try the catch of the day at Pomato Point (284-495-9466) on Anegada.

- Try any of the local fish found at the BVI Fishing Complex, a clearinghouse of seafood caught by local fishermen. Monday through Friday, 8:30 AM to 5:00 PM and on Saturdays, 8:30 AM to 1:00 PM.

- Try the fresh local catch at the Captain's Table (284-494-3885) while overlooking the Inner Harbour Marina.

- Try any of the fish specials at the Seaside Grill (284-495-4212) on the waterfront deck at Sebastian's in Apple Bay.

Marina Cay

COD FRITTERS

Ingredients:
4 oz cod
1 onion
1 clove garlic
5 chives
Fresh thyme
Fresh parsley
1 hot pepper
Salt
Pepper
2 eggs
8 oz flour
1 cup water
A pinch of baking soda
1 drop vinegar

Locals Do It Like This:
Keep the cod in cold water for approximately two hours, and then boil for thirty minutes. Let the fish cool.

Meanwhile, whisk the flour, adding the water as you go to ensure that your mixture does not become too thick or lumpy. Once the cod is cool, remove the skin and bones, and thinly mince the cod along with the onion, garlic, chives, parsley, hot pepper, and thyme. Add to the batter. Add 2 egg yolks to this mixture, and a small drop of vinegar and a pinch of baking soda. Make sure to do this just before cooking in oil. Next, dip the batter in hot oil for approximately five minutes to create fritters in small quantities.

ALSO KNOWN AS …

When you hear "pot fish" or "steak fish" there's a good chance the islander is referring to one of the many ocean-roaming fish that are often caught from local boats or charters, as well as in fish traps.

HOMETOWN HEROES YOU SHOULD KNOW:

Along with the many food finds and local goodies, it's key to know the people of the British Virgin Islands, those that make the territory truly unique. Here is a sampling; for more, visit www.islandlowdown.com.

Linnell Abbott: Linnell is the founder, publisher, and editor of The BVI Beacon. With a passion for recording—and shaping—BVI's history, Linnell manages the territory's major and most popular newspaper. Under her guidance the paper has grown from 12 pages to over 60 pages. BVIslanders praise Linnell for her total commitment to the truth and telling the story accurately and fairly.

Bert Kilbride: Though Bert now lives in California, he certainly left his mark on the islands. Bert is a diver, treasure hunter, and the owner of the original Saba Rock. Bert also owned Moskito Island and was the creator of Drake's Anchorage dive resort. Bert is most famous for his connection to Jean-Michel Cousteau, whom he led throughout the British Virgin Islands during diving and whale watching trips. Cousteau also produced a movie about Bert, solidifying this man of the sea as a hometown hero.

◇ BLONDE ROCK—BETWEEN SALT ISLAND AND PETER ISLAND

Weather permitting, you'll want to try Blonde Rock if you're lookin' for crabs. Known as an underwater amphitheater by many, this hidden spot is perfect for crabs, conch, and a variety of other species. Blonde Rock is between twenty and sixty feet deep, and boasts both large and small overhangs.

THE BEST CRAB CAKES

If you find yourself anywhere near Long Bay Beach on Tortola, make sure to check out 1748, a romantic little spot set amid an 18th-century sugar mill and surrounded by sea grape trees. Known as the "oldest new restaurant" on Tortola, 1748 boasts island favorites – such as rotis, peas and rice, and fresh-from-the-reef seafood. While choices are plentiful, just sit back, opt for the restaurant's incredible crab cakes, and take in the view of the empty beach in front of you. 1748 also offers beach-side barbecues! 1748, Tortola, (284) 495-4252.

 CARIBBEAN-STYLE CRABS

Ingredients:
1 lb crab meat, shredded
6-8 tbsp crab liquid or clam broth
8 tbsp butter
4 scallions chopped
1-2 tsp chopped garlic
1 hot green chili, finely chopped
1 tbsp curry powder
2 tbsp chopped fresh coriander leaves
2 tbsp parsley, finely chopped
BVI salt
Freshly ground pepper
2 cups bread crumbs

Locals Do It Like This:
Use a large skillet to melt the butter before adding scallions, garlic, and chili peppers. A good rule of thumb is to cook the ingredients in the skillet until the scallions are wilted. Blend the curry powder into this mixture, and then add the crab, coriander, and parsley. Add the crab liquid, along with salt and pepper, and then the bread crumbs. Place the mixture into the crab shells. Bake at 400° until golden brown (approximately 10 minutes).

BAKED SNAPPER WITH CALLALOO AND CARROT STUFFING

Ingredients:
2 lbs snapper
1 tsp black pepper
1 tsp salt

Stuffing:
1 cup water
½ cup Grace Pepper Pot Mix
2 cups carrot
¼ cup bread crumbs
1 tbsp chopped onion
1 tbsp chopped garlic
½ tsp white pepper

Locals Do It Like This:
Start by washing and deboning the fish. Create the callaloo and carrot stuffing by sautéing all seasoning ingredients, and then adding the pepper pot mix, carrots, breadcrumbs, and white pepper. Mix well. Once the snapper is stuffed with the carrot stuffing, secure the sides of the fish with skewers. Bake the fish on a greased baking sheet at 350°F for 25 minutes.

Single straw parasol shelter at Bitter End resort on Virgin Gorda.

BVI PERSPECTIVE

"Perched on a rock outcropping 90 feet above the ocean, my house overlooks eight other islands, a lush mountain-rimmed coastline that curves like a cup handle for miles, and, most importantly, the palm-fringed village of Little Apple Bay, population 125. Village life unfolds below my home with a regularity and gentility that is at times quite moving, at times a little unnerving, very often funny, but always instructive." Remar Sutton's column on the BVI's, The Washington Post, December 8, 1995.

SERIOUS ISLAND COOKS

To do it the traditional BVI way, serious island cooks always opt for coconut oil.

SERIOUS ISLAND FISHERMEN

Those serious about island cooking are serious about local fish. To meet some of the best local fishermen in BVI, head to one of the many fishing events held around the islands. The Thanksgiving Game Fish Challenge takes place on the North Sound on the weekend after Thanksgiving Day and produces wahoo, tuna, and king-fish. Likewise, the Spanish Town Fisherman's Jamboree in Spanish Town serves as an annual celebration of fishing.

BVI SALT FISH CAKE

Ingredients:
2 tbsp coconut oil
1 cup onions, finely chopped
1 cup flour
1 tsp baking powder
Salt to taste
1 egg lightly beaten
¾ cup milk
1 tbsp butter, melted
2 tbsp eschalots, finely chopped
½ lb, salted cod fish, cooked and flaked
1 large fresh hot pepper, finely chopped

Locals Do It Like This:
In a heavy frying pan, heat the oil and sauté the onions until they are just wilted. Place flour, baking powder, and salt a in bowl. Make a well in the center of the bowl and pour in the egg, butter, and milk. Mix together lightly, and then add the onions, eschalot, salted cod fish, salt, and pepper. Stir well. Drop by tbsp into hot oil, but do not crowd them in the pan.

 SCALLOPS CEVICHE

Ingredients:
1 lb scallops
1 cup lemon juice
⅓ cup lime juice
½ cup orange juice
2 tbsp ketchup
¼ tsp salt
1 cup finely chopped red onions
1 red pepper
½ of a small yellow hot chili pepper, grated or finely minced
Lettuce
⅓ cup canned corn kernels
3 or 4 sprigs cilantro
Parsley

Locals Do It Like This:
Slice scallops into strips no thicker than ⅛ inch. Place in a bowl and pour ¾ cup lemon juice over the scallops. Cover with plastic wrap and marinate at room temperature about an hour, stirring occasionally.

Meanwhile, prepare the other marinade by combining the remaining ¼ cup lemon, lime, and orange juices with ketchup, salt, onion, and finely chopped red and green peppers, and hot chili pepper.

Go back to the first marinade and drain/discard it. Remove the scallops and now cover it with the second marinade. Cover and refrigerate for five hours, turning the scallops occasionally. Place toothpicks in each scallop, garnish with finely chopped cilantro and parsley, and serve chilled over a bed of lettuce.

❚❚❚ CEVICHE PREP:

Typically, local fishermen will use yellowfin tuna, swordfish, or any combination of the two to create ceviche. They flake the fish into a strong potion of garlic, cilantro, chili powder, onions, and lime juice. Some toss in chopped tomatoes as well. Kept in the refrigerator overnight, this concoction is a perfect snack for fishermen and boaters the next day on the water.

❚❚❚ CEVICHE AT ITS FINEST

Little Dix Bay, a classic luxury resort on Virgin Gorda, offers not only a dramatic backdrop but an impressive collection of culinary creations. Head to the Beach Grill, adjacent to the resort's private dock, for a crack at their tasty ceviche along with chilled soups, tropical fruit plates, and creative cocktails. Little Dix can be reached at 284-495-5555.

CEVICHE

Ceviche, sometimes called seviche, is seafood prepared in a centuries-old method of cooking. Using acidic juice of citrus instead of heat to cook the dish, ceviche is known worldwide, especially in the Caribbean as well as Central and South America, for its many varieties.

Everyone gives ceviche a touch of individuality by adding their own garnishes—ranging from serving it with slices of cold sweet potatoes or corn on the cob to serving it with chips, nuts, toasted tortillas, or slices of raw onions.

For some, shrimp ceviche—which makes use of ketchup, some lemon, and oil like a salad—is the best. Others argue that ceviche of fish, with a hint of lemon, is unbeatable. Then there are those that opt for lobster ceviche, arguing that its mix of mayonnaise and ketchup is the most scrumptious. The point is that there is ceviche throughout the islands, but the recipes change from home to home.

Variations in the flavor of ceviche depend upon the particular citrus juice or combination of juices and other ingredients used in the marinade. The marinade can be as simple as lemon and lime. The acid in the juices, as well as the salt used in many recipes, prevents the growth of microorganisms in the fish. Giving the dish its tasty appeal, any number of hot peppers, green peppers, garlic, and onion are often added.

Classic ceviche recipe in which cubes of fresh fish are cooked by lime and lemon juice.

 SHRIMP CEVICHE

Ingredients:
2 lbs shrimp, cooked and cleaned
½ lb onions, chopped
2 tsp mustard
1½ tsp salt
½ cup olive oil
½ cup lime juice
1 hot pepper, chopped

Locals Do It Like This:
Begin by cutting the shrimp into small pieces. Mix the onions, mustard, salt, olive oil, lime juice, and hot pepper to form a marinade. Pour the marinade over the shrimp, and marinate in a covered container for eight to ten hours.

A stunning view of Jost Van Dyke.

HARDCORE CEVICHE:

On occasion, one might even spot fishermen leaving the covered mixture of freshly caught ceviche of fish in the hot Caribbean sunlight, atop a boat's outside deck to speed up the acidic action. There are even fishermen who bury their wrapped ceviche mixture just under the sand, returning to shore at lunch for the dish.

OLD SCHOOL VERSUS NEW

Old school ceviche was left to marinate for up to three hours. The modern spin on this classic though, sees a much shorter marinating period, sometimes calling for only a matter of minutes.

? CEVICHE MYTH

"Tiger Milk," the juice that remains on the plate after eating the fish, is rumored to cure hangovers.

✔ CEVICHE SNACK TIP:

Try ceviche on a tostada.

⚠ CEVICHE SAFETY

Remember: Citric acid won't kill bacteria the way that heat does when cooking. It is of utmost importance to use fresh, local, disease-free, and parasite-free fish.

━ CEVICHE TASTE TESTING

If you want to sample some of the best ceviche around, make sure to try the many variations offered by island chefs throughout the territory. Over in Cane Garden Bay, for example, Tortola is home to Myett's, (284) 495-9649, an excellent spot for conch chowder, fritters, and ceviche. Blue Iguana Catering, (284) 494-2967, another ceviche expert, is popular for dishing up their version of this classic dish, an incredible Thai calamari ceviche, during weddings and special events. And let's not forget about the Sailor's Ketch, (284) 495-2125, located at Penns Landing, where you can pick up whole or ground conch, great for ceviche, fritters, or chowder.

 HOT SHRIMP CEVICHE

Ingredients:
1 lb peeled fresh shrimp
1 onion, sliced thin
2 stalks celery, finely diced
1 aji chombo pepper, finely diced
3 limes
1 tsp fresh cilantro, minced
½ tsp sea salt
1 tbsp vegetable oil
1 tbsp garlic powder
½ tsp ground black pepper

Locals Do It Like This:
Begin by sautéing the garlic and black pepper, then add the shrimp and salt and stir. When the shrimp turns pink, add the aji chombo and other ingredients. Cover and simmer for ten minutes. Best served with boiled yucca and potatoes.

If you'd like a spicier version, cook the mixture longer, and the oils in the peppers will release into the meat.

CEVICHE OF BARRACUDA

Ingredients:
7 lbs firm white fish (i.e.; barracuda, marlin, grouper, snook or corvina)
3 large green peppers
3 tbsp salt, heaping
6 oz apple cider vinegar
4 large onions
6 hot peppers plus seeds
1 qt fresh lime juice

Locals Do It Like This:
Remove meat from the fish and dice it into ¼ inch cubes. Place cubes in a large pan.

Dice the onion, sweet peppers, and hot peppers as finely as possible. Lay the vegetables on top of the fish, then add vinegar, salt, and lime juice. Stir for approximately 5 minutes. Place mixture into a container and cover. Let stand at room temperature for one hour and then refrigerate. Ready to serve in four hours.

CEVICHE STEPPED UP A NOTCH:

Line a large glass dish or an individual serving cup (the smart money is on a wide-mouthed martini glass) with lettuce leaves. Spoon in the ceviche and garnish with rings of red onion and avocados (sliced and fanned).

CEVICHE TIMING

How long you need to marinate fish in citrus juices depends on the type of fish. Whatever the type, always cut it into bite-size strips. Flakier fillets, such as snapper and flounder, or tender shellfish like scallops, will need to marinate for approximately fifteen minutes or less. Quarter-inch strips of mahi-mahi, a hearty and dense fish, can take up to an hour to cook.

⬤ BEST BVI CEVICHE

Try your hand at the Cow Wreck Beach Ceviche at Cow Wreck (284-495-8047) Beach Bar & Grill on Anegada. Their traditional version is nothing more than fresh conch and lime. However, many locals will opt for a dash of Matouk's Hot Sauce.

⬤ THE CEVICHE MASTER: BELL CREQUE

Bell Creque and family operate the Cow Wreck Beach Bar, the home of the most talked about ceviche in all the islands. A BVI kitchen whiz, Bell is also known for her conch fritters. Cow Wreck fans, those who simply enjoy limin' at the bar, swear by Bell's tasty creations.

ESCABECHE OF FISH

Ingredients:
2 lbs fillets of any firm white fish
½ tsp garlic salt
¼ tsp white pepper
¼ tsp paprika
½ tsp curry powder
1 cup all-purpose flour
¼ cup oil
3 garlic cloves, finely chopped
3 green peppers, julienned
3 medium onions, julienned
¾ cup white vinegar
¼ cup water
1 bay leaf
Salt to taste

Locals Do It Like This:
Select a firm white fish, boned and cut into bite-size pieces. Start by seasoning the fish with curry powder, white pepper, garlic, and salt. Next, dip the pieces of fish in the flour, and fry in hot oil. Drain, and place in a glass bowl. Cook the pepper, garlic, and onions in hot oil for 5 minutes. Now place the vegetables in a bowl with the water, vinegar, salt, and bay leaf. Mix well and then pour over the fish. Let cool, and then cover before placing in the refrigerator for 24 hours. Serve cold the next day.

SHRIMP CURRY

Ingredients:
2 lbs shrimp
2 tbsp margarine
¼ cup chopped onion
2 cloves garlic, finely chopped
1 ½ tbsp flour
1 tbsp curry powder
1 tbsp lime juice
1 ½ cups lemon juice
1 ½ cups stock
¼ tsp salt
1 tsp hot pepper sauce
1 tbsp chopped parsley

Locals Do It Like This:
Heat a frying pan to melt the margarine while lightly frying onions and garlic. Slowly add the flour and curry powder while stirring. Cook for three minutes while continuing to stir. Next add lemon juice, stock, salt, and hot pepper sauce. Stir and cook for another three minutes. Add the shrimp and stir until the shrimp turns pink. Garnish with parsley.

ISLAND TIDBITS

Best Place for Fresh Fish and Shrimp:
Local fishermen bring their catches of the day to the BVI Fishing Complex in Baugher's Bay (on the outskirts of Road Town) every day! There are also fishermen who come into the villages during mid-to late-morning or in the afternoon with their goodies.

ISLAND MOVERS AND SHAKERS

Inez Archibald: The first woman to have held the position of Speaker of the Legislative Council. Inez serves as an inspiration for all BVIslanders, especially women throughout the Virgin Islands.

David Brick: The manager of Saba Rock.

Cindy Clayton: The owner of the famed Tamarind Club.

Tina Goschler: The owner of the beautiful Guavaberry Homes in Virgin Gorda.

John Rhymer: The owner of North Sound Superette Store and one heck of a pastry chef.

Lorna Smith: The Executive Director of the International Finance Center and the International Affairs Unit. Known on the islands as someone who makes things happen, Lorna has a track record for positive results in the BVI.

Joan Soncini: While not an islander, Joan is the author of one of the best books about Virgin Gorda, titled *Virgin Gorda: An Intimate Portrait* (Virgin Island Books) and has fast become a hometown hero.

🌐 ISLAND TIDBITS

Best Place for Fresh Fruit and Vegetables: There is a fruit and vegetable market on Saturday mornings at the Road Town Marketplace from 4:30 AM to 5:00 PM. Don't miss a crack at the finest produce in all of the islands!

🌐 BEST PLACE TO RECYCLE:

BVI Glass Recycling, Tortola's first recycling company, was first hatched by Mr. and Mrs. Wheatly Tomlinson after observing the amount of glass and cans thrown away after the BVI Carnival. A number of resorts, such as Peter Island Resort, have also jumped on board. Best of all, youth in the area are joining in the fun, as evidenced by the participation of the Youth Empowerment Project. BVI Recycling is located in Sea Cows Bay, Tortola. For more information, contact lwheatly@hotmail.com or call, (284) 499-1808.

 COCONUT SHRIMP

Ingredients:
Fresh shrimp
Shredded coconut
Flour
Salt
Pepper

Locals Do It Like This:
Peel and devein fresh shrimp. In a separate bowl, mix the flour, water, salt, and pepper into a thick batter. Dip the shrimp into the batter and then dab the shrimp into the shredded coconut. Next, deep-fry the coconut-covered shrimp and serve hot. For added presentation, serve the shrimp inside a coconut shell.

 CHICKEN AND BANANAS

Ingredients:
5 lbs. chicken (cut into 8 pieces)
3 tablespoons butter
3 tablespoons oil
2 onions, chopped
2 cloves garlic, minced
1 tablespoon cornstarch
1 14.5 oz. can whole tomatoes
3 carrots, diced
½ teaspoon oregano
½ teaspoon thyme
1 cup hot chicken broth
½ cup dry white wine
16 pitted prunes
6 local bananas, sliced half lengthways

Locals Do It Like This:
Preheat oven to 350°F. Meanwhile, dredge chicken pieces in flour. Then brown in two tablespoons of oil and two tablespoons of butter. Remove. Begin sautéing onions and garlic in remaining oil and butter, and add one tablespoon cornstarch mixed with water. Next add all remaining ingredients (with the exception of the bananas and the prunes), bringing to a boil. Pour over the chicken and then bake covered for 20 minutes. Finally, add the prunes and bake 20 minutes, and then add the bananas and bake for 15 additional minutes.

ISLAND CHICKEN IN GINGER WINE SAUCE

Ingredients:
1 medium sized roasting chicken
½ lb seedless white grapes
1 cup chicken stock
4 tablespoons butter
1 cup Stone's Original Green Ginger Wine
Juice of 1 lemon
2 tablespoons flour
2 tablespoons brown sugar
Freshly ground pepper and salt to taste
Fresh thyme

Locals Do It Like This:
Cut the chicken into quarters and sauté in butter until golden in color. Meanwhile, mix sliced grapes, chicken stock, lemon juice, and Stone's Original Ginger Wine sauce in a baking dish. Add ground pepper, salt, and thyme to taste. Add the chicken to the dish and bake at 350 degrees for approximately one hour and fifteen minutes. Remove the chicken, and top with brown sugar before returning to the oven until the sugar melts. Thicken the gravy with flour and pour over the chicken before serving.

ISLAND TIDBITS

Best Place for Island Chicken: At Palm's Delight (284-405-4863) you'll find the best ever "Honey-Stung Chicken." Chef Iona douses this dish with honey after it's fried! Mmmm, just when you thought it couldn't get any better, Iona next places this wonder in a ginger wine sauce.

Best Place for Pineapple: You won't find better pineapple anywhere else in the world than in the British Virgin Islands. Locals will often point to Ivan Chinnery on Jost Van Dyke as growing the best in the islands.

Best Supplier of Seafood: Since 1996, Sailor's Ketch Seafood has been known as the British Virgin Islands' best supplier of seafood to restaurants, resorts, sailors, yachtsmen, tourists, and locals.

Located on Tortola, Sailor's Ketch carries a hefty selection of locally caught Tuna, Dolphin, and Swordfish, which has become their signature. Also notable is their seasmoke dip as well as their flying fish, a down-island favorite. Sailor's Ketch offers free delivery to marinas and has retail locations at Bobby's Market Place in Road Town, Cane Garden Bay, and Nanny Cay.

Chapter Two

Straight-Up Local

❓ WHAT THE HECK IS GOAT WATER?

Often referenced around the BVI kitchen table, goat water is nothing more than curried stew. For some of the best in the islands, try Da Wedding on Tortola. With goats in abundance along the BVI's' hilly terrain, you'll find the dish popping up on many menus and popular in rotis.

🎙 WHERE TO SAMPLE GOAT WATER

The Emancipation Festival, also known as the "August Festival," is the biggest bash in BVI. Along with calypso, reggae, and costumes, partygoers get a crack at traditional dishes such as goat water, goat head soup, dove pork, pigtail, and stewed mutton.

CLASSIC GOAT WATER

Ingredients:
10 lb mutton
2 lb green pawpaw, diced
2 lb breadfruit
1 lb flour
1 lb onions
½ cup coconut oil
Gravy browning
Bouquet garni
1 lb tomatoes
6 tbsp tomato ketchup
2 oz margarine
Salt & black pepper to taste
3 bullion cubes (maggi cubes are all the rage)

Locals Do It Like This:
Start by cutting the mutton into cubes for serving bite-sized pieces. Add salt and freshly ground pepper. Lightly brown in coconut oil, then remove and place into a large pot. Simmer for 2 hours. Remove from heat and set aside.

Meanwhile, dice the breadfruit, onions, and pawpaw. Sauté these ingredients in a pan with margarine. Add this mixture to the meat and return it to a simmer. While cooking, slowly add the bouquet garni and whole peppers. Next, mix in 3 tbsp of flour, water, and gravy browning to form a paste. Add this mixture into the stew and continue to simmer. Finally, add the cubes and simmer until the meat is soft and the stew is nice and brown.

So What's Roti Anyway? Much like a sandwich or a wrap, roti is a crepe-like bread containing curry. The best in all of the BVI's is found at Roti Palace (284-494-4196) on Main Street, above Samarkand Jewelers.

Variations: There are many variations of roti, and you'll often find it served with rice as a main dish. Nothing more than curried meat, seafood, or vegetables in a crepe wrapping, many a chef has attempted to mimic the mastery of Roti Palace, but few have succeeded.

Making the Crepe: Use only unbleached white flour, baking powder, and salt. Add water to make a stiff dough before rolling into a paper-thin crepe. Make sure to spread a little corn oil before grilling.

For the Curry: Sauté onion, garlic, and ginger in butter. Add curry powder, red chilis, and vinegar to form a paste. Marinade chicken, seafood, or meat for at least two hours. Cook until tender, then fill the crepe. Serve with breadfruit.

*Explore the many colorful pastel painted storefronts throughout Tortola
—you're sure to discover local eateries serving roti.*

¡©¡ SERVE WITH …

A BVI tradition, "Rice and Peas," also known as pigeon peas or Congo peas, are really what most folks call "rice and beans." Originating in Africa, beans are often served with rice and a good-size helping of chutney or West Indian sauce spooned on top. Sounds simple enough, but rice and peas are serious business in the Caribbean— many local chefs have won a number of culinary titles with rice and peas. Rice and peas make any dish, especially curried goat, a true BVI experience.

¡©¡ SIDE ITEM TASTE TESTING

To sample the real flair of the British Virgin Islands, make sure to seek out the hidden cafes that dot the roadways and decorate the water's edge. While entrees boasting fresh fish and seasonal vegetables are all the rage, tasting the side items – such as fried plantains, sweet potatoes, cassava, and dasheen – really define the culinary culture. Take Occasions BVI, (284) 495-7313, a local catering company, which exemplifies BVI side dishes like West Indian Rice and Beans, Macaroni Pie with Cheddar and Cream, Whipped Sweet Potato with Brown Sugar and Pecan Topping, Fried Plantain, and Local Plantain Cheese Bake. Fat Hog Bob's, another side dish master in Hodges Creek, is more than a steak and rib joint. Bob's offers killer sides propped up by local veggies and island traditions. Pirates Bight, on Norman Island, is another example of island cooking where side items take center stage. At the heart of all these local joints is a reliance on native fruits and vegetables that adds an island zing to dishes like fish with fruit chutneys and spicy local stews, meat with curry sauces, and fresh produce jazzed up by ground hot pepper, nutmeg, parsley, mango, passion fruit, and papaya.

 CURRIED GOAT

Ingredients:
2 lbs mutton (or substitute with lamb) trimmed and cut into cubes
¼ cup onion, chopped
2 tbsp turmeric
2 cloves garlic, chopped
½ tsp Scotch bonnet sauce
2 tsp grated ginger
½ cup red wine
¼ tsp cooking oil
¼ tsp tomato ketchup
1 tsp curry powder
½ tsp salt
1 tsp vinegar
3 tbsp chutney

Locals Do It Like This:
Start by trimming and cutting the mutton into cubes. Add the chopped garlic, salt, vinegar, and Scotch bonnet sauce. Marinate a minimum of 1 to 2 hours. Next, heat the oil and curry powder in a skillet, and brown the meat. Add in the remaining ingredients and cover while simmering over low heat until the meat is tender. Season again before serving and place over a bed of peas and rice.

 LAMB WITH SEA GRAPE JELLY

Ingredients:
4 lamb chops
¼ pint red wine
1 onion, diced
Fresh rosemary leaves
Fresh tarragon leaves
1 tbsp olive oil
1 clove garlic
Salt and pepper to taste

Locals Do It Like This:
You'll want to start this tasty marinade twenty-four hours before serving. Begin by combining the wine, onion, rosemary, tarragon, olive oil, and garlic. Add salt and pepper to taste and then marinate the lamb chops (or lamb steaks) overnight. Grill (or fry) the lamb the next day, making sure to brush all remaining marinade on the meat as it cooks to keep it moist. The recipe is capped with a healthy serving of Sea Grape Jelly (some folks use redcurrant as a substitute).

CHEF WILLO

Like lamb? If so, try Chef "Willo" Stoutt's cinnamon-baked rack of lamb with plantains and artichokes, or his rum-basted tropical lamb satay with grilled pineapple and coconut-lime sauce. Stoutt, one of the BVIs' most celebrated culinary masterminds, oversees the very best in local eats found at Peter Island Resort. In the kitchen for close to 30 years, Chef Willo is a proud member of the gold medal-winning BVI Culinary Team and is known not only for his winning lamb recipes, but also for his knack at showcasing seasonal ingredients with beautiful presentation.

Under the guidance of Chef Willo, Peter Island Resort is popular for more than just plush digs and has made its mark through innovative cuisine – all of which is inspired by the scenery and natural elements of the island. Chef Willo taps into these influences and artfully combines international favorites with classic island eats. An incredibly personable character, Chef Willo's presence – both inside and outside of the kitchen -- adds to the overall charm of Peter Island, which also boasts secluded beaches of flour white sand, coconut palms, a breathtaking spa, and villas with private patios overlooking Big Reef Bay.

In case you've been hiding under a rock somewhere, Chef Willo and Peter Island Resort continue to receive rave reviews from the media, as evidenced by the resort making Condé Nast Traveler's "Gold List" as well as Travel + Leisure "T+L 500," which lists readers' choices for the top 500 hotels in the world. In addition, this thriving resort was named among the Top 25 Hotels in the Caribbean by Travel + Leisure in the magazine's "World's Best Awards." There are certainly a number of factors contributing to the resort's stardom, but Chef Willo's persona as well as tasty eats are headlining the growing list of the resort's credentials.

EAT LIKE A SAILOR:

Ducuna, fish and chips, steak and kidney pie, and meat pies are all popular with the standard ale and game of darts. Try them all! If you're looking for a good measuring stick, try Pusser's Pub to sample the pub grub popular among sailors while trading fish tales.

EAT ON THE RUN

Looking for local goods while on the run? Then head over to Mac's on Main Street, a local caterer with goods-to-go. Or, opt for Virgin Queen, also on Main Street. This West Indian favorite offers authentic local eats for carry-out.

DUCUNA

Ingredients:
2 sweet potatoes
½ cup sugar
2 ½ cups flour
Pinch of allspice
Pinch of cinnamon raisin

Locals Do It Like This:
Begin by grating the sweet potatoes and then adding sugar. Let the potatoes sit for one hour. Add the flour and allspice. If the mixture becomes too thick at any time, add additional water. Spoon a heaping portion of the mixture into foil paper and wrap before placing into boiling water. Boil until firm (approximately 45 minutes). Use caution when unwrapping, as it will be piping hot! Experts often serve Ducuna with a hefty plate of salt fish—mmmmm.

COCONUT CHIPS

Ingredients:
1 ripe coconut
Salt

Locals Do It Like This:
Open the ripe (hard) coconut and drain the water inside. Next, wrap the drained coconut in a towel, and smash with a blunt object into five or more pieces. Begin carving the coconut meat from the shell with a knife (be careful) and remove any of the brown skin from the meat. If the coconut meat is difficult to remove, bake the coconut pieces for fifteen minutes at 375° and then attempt removal again. Once removed, cut the coconut pieces into paper-thin chips, place them on a baking sheet, and sprinkle with salt. Bake at 350° for eight minutes, turning frequently until golden in color.

BVI STYLE LOBSTER SALAD

Ingredients:
2 tbsp fresh lemon juice
½ cup mayonnaise
12 oz cooked lobster
¼ cup cucumber, diced
¼ cup onion, chopped
¼ cup celery, chopped
¼ cup green pepper, chopped
Salt and pepper
A touch of Scotch bonnet sauce

Locals Do It Like This:
Mix the mayonnaise and juice together, then add the lobster (setting aside the lobster tail shell), cucumber, onion, celery, and green pepper. Toss together. Serve immediately inside the lobster tail or chill for later. Add a drop of Scotch bonnet if you'd like, and serve with a lemon chunk on the side.

 FRIED FLYING FISH

Ingredients:
2 pounds flying fish fillets
2 eggs
1½ cups flour
¼ cup onion (minced)
2 teaspoons fresh thyme (minced)
2 tablespoons parsley (minced)
1 teaspoon celery leaves (minced)
1 teaspoon Worcestershire sauce
Salt
Freshly ground black pepper
Coconut oil

Locals Do It Like This:
Form a batter by combining the eggs, flour, onion, thyme, parsley, celery leaves, Worcestershire sauce, black pepper, and salt. Add the flying fish to the batter and marinate for sixty minutes. Fry the flying fish in oil until golden brown. Serve with local hot sauce.

LOBSTER LOWDOWN:

Where's the best? Anegada, enough said!

Searching for the best Anegada lobster and other eats?

Then you'll need a good cabbie! You'll want to ask for Mitch when you first arrive on the "sunken island." Mitch has lived on the island his entire life and besides being an all-around-good-guy, he'll turn out to be your all-around-go-to-guy. He'll give you an island tour, make deliveries, and fill you in on all of the island's sip-sip (gossip).

FLYING FISH LOWDOWN

For a killer flying fish sandwich, try Foxy's Tamarind Bar (284-495-9258) on Jost Van Dyke. Wash it down with Foxy's Painkiller.

⬗ A PINCH OF "SEASONINGS"

Most often this phrase means any number of local combination bouquets of thyme, parsley, ginger root, bay leaves, allspice, tied rolls of cinnamon bark, and other local herbs found in Caribbean markets.

⬗ OLD FAVORITES

Plenty of seasonings are always at hand in any island kitchen. Many popular low-cost dishes are jazzed up with just the right touch of local spices. Whitefish, known as "ole wife" and "doctors," is a traditional meal served with seasonings. "Porgies and grunts," another local fave, really pops when the right seasonings are added to yellowtail, kingfish, lobster, wahoo, grouper, mahi-mahi, tuna, and bonito.

 OKRA 'N' RICE

Ingredients:
2 cups rice
1 onion
2 cups okra
½ cup celery
½ cup salt pork
6 oz tomato paste
Thyme and parsley
Salt and pepper
Scotch bonnet sauce
4 cups water

Locals Do It Like This:
Chop up the salt pork, onion, celery, and okra. Combine these ingredients and fry until a light golden brown. Next, add the tomato paste and continue to cook for approximately five more minutes or until the mixture returns to a brownish color. Combine the thyme, parsley, rice, and hot sauce with four cups of water and bring to a boil. Reduce heat and simmer for up to one hour or until rice is done.

Check to make sure all of the water is soaked up and season again before serving.

OXTAIL STEW AND BUTTER BEANS

Ingredients:
2 ½ lbs oxtail
4 tsp corn flour
2 tbsp vegetable oil
1 tbsp salt
2 tbsp black pepper
4 strips of bacon, sugar cured
2 onions
1 clove garlic
4 carrots
1 cup tomatoes, chopped
½ liter hot water
2 stalks escallion
1 fresh sprig thyme
2 cans butter beans

Locals Do It Like This:
Begin by cutting the oxtail into small pieces and trimming away any excess fat. Boil the oxtail in water for three minutes. Meanwhile, slice the carrots, onions, and scallion thinly. Next, chop the tomatoes and crush the garlic. Remove the oxtail from the water and dry before coating with corn flour. In a separate pot, heat oil and add the oxtail. Brown the oxtail on both sides and then remove. Next fry the bacon in thin slices. Return the oxtail back to the pot with the bacon, and add the carrot, onion, garlic, tomatoes, and hot water. Uncover and check the tenderness of the oxtail (it should almost be tender). Add seasonings to taste and return to a simmer (covered) for an additional twenty minutes. Finally, add the butter beans and simmer for the last three minutes.

❧ BVI VOICES

"In our little village, within walking distance of a small, fancy hotel, one friend makes do on the sale of a few island limes and sweet potatoes each day. Close by, another sells homemade bread, and next door an important church leader greets a passerby as her ax takes off the head of a goat—the beginning of a favorite soup and fine curried stew." Remar Sutton, *The Washington Post*, December 8, 1995.

HISTORY OF CALLALOO

Almost always made with okra, callaloo has a distinctively Caribbean origin created by African slaves. There are many variations, including Caribbean lobster, chili peppers, crab, and coconut milk. To make the best callaloo in all of the BVI, you'll want to seek out healthy green dasheen leaves with a large purple dot. For a substitute, try Swiss chard, spinach, or kale.

CALLALOO IN PRINT:

Eighteen writers from both the British and United States Virgin Islands have hatched *Virgin Islands Callaloo*, an impressive collection of poems from the Caribbean by Callaloo Poets. The publication resulted from a series of poetry readings by the Indigo Society, and it was officially launched by the Department of Culture in the BVI. To order a copy of *Virgin Islands Callaloo*, visit www.authorhouse.com.

CALLALOO CRAB SOUP

Ingredients:
¼ lb pickled crab meat
3 crabs
1 dozen Callaloo (dasheen) leaves
1 tbsp butter
8 ochroes
1 pint boiling water
1 celery stalk
1 clove garlic
½ lb shrimp (optional)
1 onion
Salt and pepper
1 Scotch bonnet (optional)

Locals Do It Like This:
Cut the pickled meat while boiling the crabs. Wash and cut the ochroes, onion, celery, and garlic. Add all ingredients into boiling water and simmer for 45 minutes. Remove the crabs from the pot. Add the crab meat to the soup before serving.

ALL THINGS CALLALOO

Callaloo, the Caribbean version of gumbo, is also known as calalú, calulul, and caruru. Typical callaloo seasonings include garlic, scallions, Scotch bonnet pepper, and thyme. The other ingredients usually include cooked ham, bacon, onions, bell peppers, and tomatoes.

For an exotic presentation, use whole crabs and include them in the pot to cook. Or add lobster medallions to the pot for a gourmet twist. Make your own broth or stock by simmering fish bones, chicken, or meat to make a sauce and adding a bouquet of seasonings, celery, and onion.

While canned callaloo leaves can be found among Caribbean markets, Swiss chard and fresh spinach are common substitutions if you can't use callaloo.

Best Place for Callaloo: The Crab Hole, on Virgin Gorda, serves up a mean version of West Indian callaloo, with tasty johnnycakes to boot.

Nothing says Caribbean cooking like callaloo.

"Calaloo, Strange Calaloo
Mysterious curious roux
Try as you might to avoid the hoodoo
Sooner or later we're all in the stew
We got crab and pigtail
Squid ink and fish scale
Okra and dasheen leaves
Chitchat and chatter
Fill up the platter
With a garnish of pure make-believe"

-Jimmy Buffett, "Callaloo" from *Don't Stop the Carnival*

 CALLALOO FRITTERS

Ingredients:
2 cups raw callaloo
½ onion
1 tomato
2 tbsp margarine
1 cup flour
1 tbsp baking powder
1 egg
Coconut oil
Salt

Locals Do It Like This:
Cut the callaloo into pieces and steam it for five to ten minutes. Cool and set aside. Meanwhile, melt the margarine in a sauté pan, adding the chopped onion and tomato. Beat the egg and add it to the cooling callaloo. Next combine the flour, baking powder, and salt in a separate bowl. Add the egg and callaloo into the flour mixture. In a frying pan filled with half of an inch of cooking oil, add the mixture (one tbsp at a time) and fry.

TIPS TO COOK LIKE AN ISLANDER:

⌒ Create a Creole sauce by combining bell peppers with garlic and sautéed onions and tomatoes.

⫿ Always use callaloo seasonings (garlic, scallions, thyme and a Scotch bonnet pepper).

🍽 Remember that many of these island ingredients can be eaten raw; the cooking process is simply to infuse ingredients.

☛ Always make your own homemade broth when creating sauces—a hefty dose of shallots, roasted garlic, and chive sticks is always a good bet. Traditional island chefs will combine these ingredients as they boil and simmer chicken, meat, or fish bones to make a tasty sauce.

🐚 When making salsa omit the tomatoes, and replace with tropical fruits, beans, and avocados.

☛ Use Sofrito, a sauce made from cilantro and other seasonings, along with pork and ham.

🥄 When using cooking oil, always opt for coconut oil.

🔥 Use only local wood or charcoal at all times. Barbecuing with a local wood from Anegada, called torch, is unbeatable.

The essence of BVI cooking is found in the use of fresh local ingredients and the reliance on local farmers.

BREADFRUIT DEFINED

Serving as a staple food, breadfruit is a fixture in the BVI culinary scene. Rich in starch, breadfruit can be baked, boiled, roasted, or fried. Potato-like in taste, breadfruit can be eaten once cooked or further processed into a number of other foods.

BVI Breadfruit, a large shady tree, is found in groves throughout the islands. To sample the islands' best, head to town on Saturday morning to peruse the local market. Or if you're extremely lucky, you might convince Egberth Donovan at the North Shore Shell Museum to let you sample some breadfruit from his own tree.

CHEERS TO YOU, CAPT. BLIGH

Breadfruit was brought to the Caribbean by the infamous Captain Bligh and the HMS Bounty, who were tasked with collecting the plant from Tahiti and Timor in an effort to transport it to the Caribbean to feed slaves in 1778. Now an island favorite, breadfruit is extremely nutritious and energy producing. In fact, breadfruit trees, which produce fruit year round, can be spotted in many local gardens and yards. The pulp of fresh breadfruit consists of 70% water, but when dried its composition resembles wheat flour and is therefore used as a substitute in many tropical regions where there is a lack of bread-producing grains. Thanks to Captain Bligh, breadfruit is now eaten raw, cooked, roasted, or fried into chips. Additionally, it can be used to make massage ointments, and its leaves can be brewed into tea (to control high blood pressure), ear drops, and into an ash that can be rubbed onto skin infections.

BREADFRUIT SOUP

Ingredients:
8 oz of beef or pork (beef cut from the round, flank, shank, and plate—cut into smaller pieces)
1 ripe breadfruit
16 oz coco
3 tbsp coconut oil
3 liters water
1 cup carrots
1 ripe papaya (make sure it's green!)
1 cup sweet pepper
1 cup tomatoes
Salt to taste
¼ tsp fresh ground black pepper
1 tsp hot pepper sauce
1 onion

Locals Do It Like This:
Cut the meat into small pieces. Next peel and cube the breadfruit. Add the coco, carrots, and green papaya along with the chopped onion and sweet pepper. In a skillet, brown the meat in the cooking oil and then add to a larger pot. Add all of the ingredients and bring to a boil. Reduce heat and cover. Continue to simmer over low heat until the meat is tender (about 45 minutes). Season this hearty soup to taste before serving. Serve with wafer crackers.

BREADFRUIT PIE

Ingredients:
1 breadfruit
½ lb grated cheese
2 tbsp mustard
1 tsp salt
1 tbsp bread crumbs
2 tbsp flour
½ oz butter
½ onion
1 ¾ cup milk
1 egg

Locals Do It Like This:
Peel and cut the breadfruit lengthwise and then divide into sections, removing the core. Boil the breadfruit in salt water. Meanwhile, slice the onion thinly, and then create a thick cheese sauce using the grated cheese, milk, flour, and margarine. Remove the breadfruit pieces from the boiling water and cool. Next, place the breadfruit in a greased pie dish, topping it with the cheese sauce and onion. Stir the ingredients lightly and top with breadcrumbs. Bake until brown (approximately 15 minutes).

Breadfruit can be baked, grilled, fried, boiled, or roasted.

MEDICINAL PURPOSES

Breadfruit leaves, Artocarpus Altilis, can be used for high blood pressure. The leaves, when slightly crushed, can also be bound on the forehead as a cure for headaches.

OTHER BREADFRUIT CREATIONS

Breadfruit is found in a number of excellent island recipes: breadfruit casserole, breadfruit cheese pie, breadfruit soup, breadfruit roll with fish filling, breadfruit chips, breadfruit scones, and breadfruit with corned beef stuffing.

TRY CHEF LORI'S VERSION

Mike and Lori Vivant, who are both United States Coast Guard (USCG) Master Captains and Dive Instructors, are often found during the winter months crewing the Millennium, a popular catamaran that serves all meals, beverages, and just about every water sport imaginable. Lori, who attended Bon Vivant School of Cooking, knows the best way to get the party started aboard the Millennium is with her tasty shrimp and mango tostada salad. With two dives a day featuring the BVI's' best underwater playgrounds, you'll want to save time for Chef Lori's creative and always seasonal menu. For more info, call 1-800-811-1475 or e-mail ginnyn@catamaransailing.com.

 SHRIMP AND MANGO SALAD

Ingredients:
1 cabbage
1 lb shrimp
2 cups plain yogurt
1 fresh sprig of parsley
3 mangoes, only half ripe
1 tsp lime juice
1 tsp Scotch bonnet sauce (optional)
¼ tsp salt

Locals Do It Like This:
Begin by cutting the shrimp in half and deveining. Next shred the cabbage, cut the pepper into strips, and peel the mango and cut it into strips as well. Combine the vegetables, shrimp, and mango and toss. Add in the yogurt, parsley, and lime juice. Add a touch of hot pepper sauce (optional). Chill for thirty minutes before serving.

JOHNNY CAKE

Ingredients:
¼ cup vegetable shortening
2 cups flour
¼ cup sugar
½ tablespoon baking powder
1½ ounces margarine
1 egg
3 ounces evaporated milk
2 to 4 tablespoons water as needed
Pinch of salt
Vegetable oil heated for deep frying

Locals Do It Like This:
Add all of the ingredients to the flour. Mix dough well and roll with sprinkled flour into balls that are approximately 2½ inches in diameter. Flatten to a thickness of about half an inch with a rolling pin. Drop each (one at a time) into the hot oil and fry until dark golden brown on all sides. Remove from frying pan and blot with a paper towel to remove excess oil. Serve hot or at room temperature.

Recipe courtesy of Cynthia Rose.

BVI BANANA AND MANGO BREAD

Ingredients:
2 ripe bananas, mashed
1 ripe mango, peeled and pureed
1 cup butter
1 ¼ cup brown sugar
3 eggs
3 cups flour (use cake or pastry flour)
½ tsp salt
½ tsp cinnamon
¼ tsp fresh nutmeg
1 cup golden raisins
½ cup walnuts, chopped

Locals Do It Like This:
Cream the butter in a bowl, combining with the sugar until fluffy. Add the eggs and beat. Set the bowl aside. Combine the cake flour, cinnamon, nutmeg, and salt in another bowl. Mash the bananas with the mango puree and combine in the bowl with the flour mixture. Next, add the two bowls together (the banana/flour mixture with the creamed butter mixture). Fold the raisins and walnuts into the batter, then pour the batter into a greased loaf pan (8 ½ by 4 ½ works best). Bake at 350° for approximately one hour. Let cool in the pan for ten minutes before removing.

Y BIG BANANA TAKES ON THIS LOCAL CLASSIC

Big Banana (284-495-4606), also called the "Paradise Club" in Cane Garden Bay, takes a different spin on the classic banana bread recipe. Though the club may be known best for its Big Banana house drink (rum, Bailey's, coconut cream, and a banana), locals know to wake up early for the pub's scrumptious coconut banana bread recipe.

BANANA MANGO SMOOTHIE

Try combining three local bananas with two mangoes, ¼ cup of coconut milk, and 1 tablespoon of honey. Blend with ice for a perfect island concoction.

MEDICINAL MANGOES

Mangoes, which are rich in anti-oxidant vitamins, can help with everything from arteriosclerosis to diabetes. Mangoes produce a positive effect on high blood pressure and the arteries, and they help prevent circulatory complications. They are diuretic and bursting with potassium while low in sodium. Mangoes are also helpful for eczema, dermatosis, skin dryness, premature aging, and retinal conditions.

THE "BEST" AWARDS

Best Place for Coconut Bread: Cline's Bakery (284-495-4549). Mrs. Cline will make the best coconut bread you've ever tasted! If you have room, pick up a guava pie while you're there.

Best Place for Fried Cauliflower and Plantain: Garden Restaurant (284-495-4931). Served on a picture-perfect deck overlooking the bay, the best fried cauliflower and plantains are found at Garden Restaurant. The popular chef makes this dish from scratch, and it shows!

Best Place for Banana French Toast: Peter Island Resort (284-495-2000). You'll find one of the best variations on French toast on this tiny private island. Make sure to add their signature tamarind syrup.

Best Place for Rum French Toast: Sugar Mill on the Gazebo Terrace (284-495-4355). Alfresco breakfast dinning doesn't get much better than this.

Best Place for Curried Soup: Sugar Mill (284-495-4355). Though they're famous for the Peanut Pumpkin Soup, Sugar Mill's Curried Soup is the real showstopper. The chef is quite possibly the BVI master of international cuisine.

Best Place for Conch "Souse" Salad: Bitter End (284-494-2746). This clubhouse, with its dark décor, has mastered ceviche and it shows in their "Souse" salad.

A breathtaking view of the British Virgin Islands.

PLANTAINS

Ingredients:
2 large green plantains
½ cup breadcrumbs
1 egg
Salt
2 tbsp peanut butter
1 onion, minced
A stick of celery
½ cup milk

Locals Do It Like This:
Cook plantains and crush while still hot. Add the breadcrumbs, egg, salt, peanut butter, minced onion and celery. Blend well and then add to a baking dish. Bake for 25 minutes.

CARIBBEAN FRIED SHRIMP

Ingredients:
1 lb. shrimp (shelled and deveined)
1 egg
2 tablespoons water
1 teaspoon fresh lime juice
Scotch bonnet peppers to taste
⅔ cups yellow cornmeal
Salt
1 teaspoon curry powder
½ tsp. garlic powder
¼ tsp. paprika
Coconut oil

Locals Do It Like This:
Beat the egg with water, add the freshly squeezed lime juice, and crush in the hot peppers. Next, in a separate dish combine the cornmeal, salt, and all seasonings. Dip the shelled and deveined shrimp into the egg mixture, and then dredge in the cornmeal until coated. Fry the shrimp until golden brown.

▮◉▮ MIDTOWN RESTAURANT DOES PLANTAINS RIGHT

Smack dab in the heart of Road Town on Main Street, this local watering hole has mastered the art of fried plantains. A popular local hangout, they serve plantains, fungi, or Caribbean carrots with almost every dish. This side item of choice for most BVIslanders is often served with curried chicken and mutton, conch soup, boiled bull-foot soup, chicken roti, or jerk chicken. Midtown Restaurant (284-494-2764).

▮◉▮ THE PUB DOES FRIED SHRIMP RIGHT

The Pub, a rustic dockside watering hole (you can dinghy right up), is perfect for fried shrimp. Better yet, try the chef's combo platter which includes fried shrimp, spareribs, and chicken. The Pub is at the southern edge of Road Town's harbor on Tortola. (284-494-2608).

ALL THINGS FUNGI
Fungi Defined

Much like a West African mash, fungi is most often served as a side dish made of cornmeal. BVI chefs differentiate fungi by using coconut milk instead of water. Made from scratch by locals, the best fungi is served as a slice with okra, onions, or sweet peppers.

To Make Fungi

Many island cooks will mix ¼ cup of cornmeal and ¾ cup of water in a small bowl. They then add this mixture to boiling water while slowly adding more cornmeal and stirring lovingly. Boiled okra and other items are sometimes folded in. Butter, salt, and pepper are also added. Next, serious chefs will "double-boil" the concoction in a large pot, stirring often. The thick pudding-like substance can be transferred into a greased bowl and formed into a ball, sliced and served hot, or meat and fish can be included on the side.

Historical Significance

Fungi is widely known as the unofficial dish of the Virgin Islands. During the days of slavery, Danish law allowed each slave six salt herring and six quarts of cornmeal per week. African women used their creative talents to turn these rations into fish and fungi, a fine dish that is enjoyed today throughout the islands. Occasionally, there were other foods thrown into the ration like yams and other vegetables, but the mainstay of cornmeal and fish led the African women to the creative result of fish and fungi.

But I Thought Fungi Was Music?

Yes, fungi is also a name given to the indigenous BVI style of music that is popular for its homegrown combo of musical instruments like washboards and gourds. One of the most well known fungi artists in BVI is Elmore Stoutt, who many islanders regard as the "Fungi Master."

Who Does Fungi Right?

If you're looking for the best fungi dish, check out Clem's by the Sea (284-495-4350) for a crack at authentic fish and fungi. Go on a Monday night for live music as an added bonus.

Other Spots for Good Fungi

If you're still in the mood for even more fungi, try Midtown Restaurant (284-494-2764), as most of the local fare served here comes with a side of fungi. While these hometown heroes prep fungi the traditional way, there are also several luxury resorts that provide a gourmet twist. The Bitter End, for example, is known to offer guava lamb with fungi.

CASSAVA AND COCONUT PONE

Ingredients:
3 lbs cassava
1 dry coconut
1 ½ pumpkin
1 can evaporated milk (1 cup)
1 vanilla bean
1 ¼ lbs butter
Cinnamon
Nutmeg

Locals Do It Like This:
Begin by grating the coconut, cassava, and pumpkin, and then mixing together. Next, cut the vanilla bean in half and empty its contents into the mixture. Add the milk and butter, and season the mixture with a touch of freshly ground nutmeg and cinnamon. Place the mixture into a greased pan and bake at 350° for one hour.

PAN FRIED CASSAVA BREAD

Ingredients:
1 cup fresh cassava meal (grated, dried cassava)
1½ teaspoons all purpose flour
1 teaspoon baking powder
1 tablespoon sugar (optional)
1 egg
¾ cup milk
1 tablespoon coconut oil
1 teaspoon lime juice

Locals Do It Like This:
Begin by mixing together all of the dry ingredients. Next, add the egg and milk to create a thick batter before stirring in the oil and lime juice. Pour your tasty batter into a greased frying pan and begin to cook over moderate heat for ten minutes; then turn over and cook for an additional three minutes. Be careful to make sure the bread does not burn at the bottom. Serve cold.

BVISLANDERS LOVE THEIR CASSAVA

Cassava, also known as Yucca and manioc, is a staple in the BVI diet and is the main crop produced (along with bananas and sweet potatoes). Slender with bark-like skin, cassava has a starchy flesh and is often served like a potato. Island chefs are also adept at turning the popular cassava into bread, chips, and sometimes they serve it with sweet pone (pudding) cake or pie as a popular desert.

CASSAVA ON DISPLAY

Not long ago a cassava griddle was unearthed at Belmont Point on Tortola, proving once again the love for cassava found among islanders. The griddle, believed to have been used by the Arawaks, is now on display at the Virgin Island Folk Museum in Road Town.

⦿ A DIFFERENT VARIATION ON CRAB

While Tropical Voodoo and its tasty spin on the use of crab in a recipe may be truly tasty, Jolly Roger at Soper's Hole is the master of tweaking crab creations. Take for instance Chef Louis' Habanero-scented crab cakes, a popular treat at the West End, Tortola local stomping grounds (also an excellent spot for nightlife). Make sure to pop in and ask Louis about this hard-to-beat crab recipe. Jolly Roger at Soper's Hole in West End, Tortola, (284-495-4599).

⦿ THE TRADITIONAL CRAB CAKE

For crab cakes the old-fashioned way, drop by De Loose Mongoose, a spunky little beach bar on the southeast corner of Trellis Bay. The portions are generous and the crab cakes are topped off with an unbelievable dipping sauce. De Loose Mongoose's proximity to the airport makes this spot a favorite for vacationers looking to kill a little time before their flight home. For those lucky enough to stay, however, the bar offers a lively Sunday night BBQ with live entertainment by MJ Blues. (284-495-2303)

 TROPICAL VOODOO

Ingredients:
2 lbs crab meat
2 tbsp coconut oil
3 scallions
2 cloves garlic
2 sprigs fresh thyme
½ lb bacon
1 lb callaloo
1 lb okra
3 limes
1 Scotch bonnet chili
8 cups water
Salt and pepper

Locals Do It Like This:
Begin by browning the crab along with chopped garlic, scallions, and thyme. Dice the bacon into small pieces and add the bacon, okra, and callaloo into a large stockpot. Add the water and cook for approximately twenty minutes. Make sure to stir while adding salt, black pepper, and the juice of three limes.

BVI BAKED CRAB

Ingredients:
1 lb cooked crab meat
2 eggs
4 tbsp melted butter
Bread crumbs
Salt and black pepper
Scotch bonnet hot pepper sauce to taste

Locals Do It Like This:
Mix together the crab, butter, eggs, and spices. Create small circular cakes (flat) and roll into the breadcrumbs. Fry on both sides until golden brown. Lobster meat can be substituted as a tasty variation. Scotch bonnet sauce is optional.

 CRAB-STUFFED DEVILED EGGS

Ingredients:
6 ounces crabmeat, flaked
8 hardboiled eggs, peeled
2 teaspoons cider vinegar
3 tablespoons mayonnaise
½ teaspoon fresh thyme, chopped
½ teaspoon hot sauce
¼ teaspoon Dijon-type mustard
Local salt and fresh ground black pepper
Fresh parsley
Hot sauce

Locals Do It Like This:
Start by cutting the eggs in half (lengthwise) and removing the yolks. Place the yolks in a bowl and mash, and then sprinkle in the vinegar. Next, combine the thyme, mustard, and mayonnaise. Finally, mix the crab and season to taste. Scoop one tablespoon of the crab mixture into the cavity of each egg-white half. Garnish with parsley. Some add a dash of hot sauce.

DID YOU KNOW?

From the basic crab cake and conch fritter to cutting-edge fusion cuisine, Tortola is the hub of all things gastronomic! In fact it's home to a branch of the New England Culinary Institute. This culinary hotspot, in partnership with the H. Lavity Stoutt Community College (HLSCC), has cranked out numerous culinary masters, in part due to the local flavors and fresh Caribbean ingredients available to students.

To get a sampling of student creations, try a few of these locations: Fort Burt Restaurant in Road Town, Road Town Bakery on Main Street, and The College Cafeteria found on campus.

New England Culinary Institute at HLSCC Fort Burt Restaurant (284-4942587)

Road Town Bakery (284-494-0222)

☞ LOCAL PUMPKIN SOUP

Skyworld, perched on one of Tortola's loftiest peaks, sits 1,300-plus feet above the remaining British Virgin Islands. Offering sweeping views, this popular eatery is home to the island's best pumpkin soup, a house favorite that is always thick and creamy with a hint of coconut and island spices. Often changing their menu, Skyworld offers a rotating selection of other homemade soups that feature peaches, coconuts, melons, and champagne. 284-494-3567.

 PUMPKIN SOUP, ISLAND STYLE

Ingredients:
2 tablespoons olive oil
2 small onions, chopped (about 2 cups)
2 celery stalks, chopped
2 small carrots, cut into thin rounds
1 quarter size slice ginger, peeled and cut into matchsticks
6 fresh thyme sprigs
5 cups pumpkin, peeled and cubed (about 2 ½ pounds)
4 to 4 ½ cups chicken broth
⅛ teaspoon freshly grated nutmeg
⅛ teaspoon allspice
1 tablespoon light brown sugar
½ cup heavy cream or half and half
½ cup unsweetened coconut milk

Locals Do It Like This:
Heat oil in soup pot. Over medium heat, sauté onion, celery, carrot, ginger and thyme until soft, approximately 6 to 8 minutes. Add cubed pumpkin and chicken broth to barely cover vegetables. Bring to a boil, reduce heat and simmer, covered, until pumpkin is very soft, anywhere from 20 to 30 minutes, depending on size of cubes. Remove cover; add brown sugar, nutmeg and allspice. Cool.

In batches, puree vegetables in a blender, adding only enough broth to blend easily. Continue to add broth to reach desired consistency. Soup should be on the thick side.

Return puree to soup pot. Add cream and coconut milk. Heat through and serve hot.

Courtesy of Donna Arter, Chef and Director, Hawks Nest Management Ltd, Tortola, British Virgin Islands

LOOKING FOR INGREDIENTS

Without a doubt, the best place to start gathering ingredients for any local recipe is at a farmers' market. One of the largest can be found every Saturday morning in Road Town, Tortola. This hot spot for all things local attracts growers from all over the islands. If you can't find something, just ask; local farmers are more than happy to fill you in on what's in season. If you must, you can also find the ingredients you need for local recipes at many grocers:

Bobby's Marketplace in Road Town (284-494-2189 or www.bobbysmarketplace.com is open 365 days a year and offers just about every ingredient under the Caribbean sun. Free pickup and delivery is offered; they also have an easy online ordering system. Bobby also runs equally reputable gigs out of both Nanny Cay and Cane Garden Bay.

Ample Hamper on Tortola (284-494-2494 or www.amplehamper.com) has three locations with a wide variety of ingredients and supplies. Online ordering makes provisioning easy, and free delivery is offered anywhere on Tortola.

Buck's Food Market on Virgin Gorda (284-495-5423) sits at the water's edge of Yacht Harbor, offering a large cross section of groceries, an in-store bakery, and a deli.

Port Purcell Market on Tortola is always a good bet, (284) 494-2724.

Rosy's Enterprises on Virgin Gorda is a favorite for countless islanders and tourists alike, (284) 495-5245.

Faulkner's Country Store on Anegada sits behind a little white picket fence in Village Square. You'll be treated to a quaint country store with local ingredients and island fare (plantains, pigtail, and lots of local veggies), along with tons of local lowdown.

Riteway Food Markets have been a popular choice in BVI since 1977. Riteway offers five retail stores, two wholesale outlets, and a cash-and-carry option. For more lowdown, call their main line at 284-494-2263, or for provisioning, fax them at 284-494-7460.

TICO is your kind of place if you're on the hunt for lots of fine booze. Plus, it boasts a large variety of wine and spirits on the cheap. Keep an eye out for specials and regular promos. (284-494-2211)

Comissary is not only a good spot for sandwiches and soup, but also a wealth of groceries for those in Yacht Harbour. (284-495-5834)

Water Tanks: In addition to local eats and ingredients, many seek out a good location to refill water tanks. Locations to refill tanks include Saba Rock, Soper's Hole, North Sound at the Bitter End, Virgin Gorda Yacht Harbour in "The Valley," Marina Cay, Leverick Bay, and Biras Creek.

WHO IS MISS MERMAID?

As the most popular BVI blogger, Miss Mermaid has dazzled islanders and tourists alike with tales of the tropics, family recipes, and informative weather reports for over ten years. Though her identity is kept top secret, fans can't get enough of her writings on "life in a strange island world." The Dear Miss Mermaid web-site, which was originally started as a place to report weather, quickly morphed into her insightful writings on island life and what she calls, "the comedy of living on the edge of reason in the Caribbean." From Calypso Casserole and Caribbean Rum Cake to "Mermaid Jokes" and a helpful island directory, Miss Mermaid offers a clearinghouse of all things BVI! In recent years, Miss Mermaid has also created a colorful calendar highlighting BVI's most stunning tropical flowers. Locals and tourists routinely keep tabs on Miss Mermaid at www.dearmissmermaid.com.

WHO IS THE BRITISH VIRGIN ISLANDS HERITAGE CONSERVATION GROUP?

Dedicated to providing information on the history of the British Virgin Islands, this beloved conservation group calls for responsible development and encourages others to get involved in their mighty efforts. Their motivation is fueled by the fact that the BVI population of approximately twenty-two thousand is now overwhelmed by upwards of three hundred thousand visitors each year. Led by BVI citizens and residents, and supported by visitors to the islands, the British Virgin Islands Heritage Conservation Group (BVIHCG) is passionate about the preservation of the BVI's natural resources, history, and culture, which many feel is threatened by today's island-wide construction. The BVIHCG team instead supports smaller, eco-friendly sustainable development with the least environmental and socioeconomic impact to the community. Activities have included "Save Beef Island" and "Save Smugglers Cove" rallies, with an energized crowd and information shared on development projects that some feel will threaten the integrity of BVI. Such festivities typically include T-shirts, passionate islanders reading poetry, and speakers urging the public to stand up for their children's future. The BVIHCG provides well-documented research papers, an active forum, and the latest on proposed development projects throughout BVI at www.bvichg.com.

WHAT IS THE MANGROVE ACTION PROJECT?

Fueled by the fact that over 80 percent of the mangroves in the British Virgin Islands have already been lost, the Mangrove Action Project encourages others to consider the excessive environmental costs of the many large-scale development projects currently underway. The Mangrove Action Project is but one of many groups now advocating for smart growth and pointing to the fact that there are far-reaching social consequences of mega-development projects.

WHAT IS PRESERVING NATURE'S SECRETS?

Preserving Nature's Secrets is a popular film produced and shot by Ben Knight and Travis Rummel, the founding partners of Felt Sole Media. Still enjoying critical acclaim from their 2005 film, The Hatch, a flyfishing/conservation documentary, this dynamic duo has now directed their camera on the British Virgin Islands and plans for large-scale developments that will change the character and the environment of the country. The film focuses on the people and places that make BVI unique, while exploring how to continue to lure visitors from around the world by preserving and strengthening the area's natural beauty.

Chapter Three

The Pantry &
Condiments

AS SEEN AROUND THE ISLANDS

BREADFRUIT *(Artocarpus altilis)* Found in abundance decorating the local breadfruit tree, this starchy island favorite is perfect for local meat dishes. Brought over by the infamous Captain Bligh from the South Pacific in the 1700s, breadfruit was often used as food for slaves. Quickly gaining favor for its versatility, BVIslanders now roast it, broil it, and bake it. Best of all, breadfruit is available all year round. Locals know that breadfruit can be treated as a potato or it can be added to a favorite soup, while others simply dice it and fry up a crispy treat.

PLANTAIN *(Musa paradisiaca)* A common addition to any BVI dish, plantains are a favorite food of the tropics and used in every meal from breakfast to dinner. With its white and pulpy insides, the plantain is most often sliced and fried in butter over low heat until golden brown.

SOURSOP *(Annona muricata)* One of the best kept secrets of the islands, soursop can make the creamiest drink or shake in town. Dark green on the outside with tiny spikes, the pulpy insides are easily mashed and blended for tasty creations.

SUGAR APPLE *(Annona squamosa)* Similar to a soursop, but sweeter, the sugar apple is often eaten plain— it's that good, and sweet! When ripe, a little applied pressure will cause the sugar apple's segments to separate, exposing the sweet insides.

COCONUT *(Cocis nucifera)* Here's a tip: if the outer husk of a coconut looks green, it's unripe. But if it's brown, it's ready to eat. However, purists know that the riper the coconut, the less milk it will produce. Translation: If you're looking to make a quick drink, go green.

Coconuts decorate a palm tree on Cane Garden Bay Beach, Tortola.

GUAVA *(Psidium guajava)* Found in just about every tropical punch, a ripe guava is like gold in the Caribbean. Yellow on the outside and bright orangey pink on the inside, guava nectar is unforgettable! Aromatic and juicy, guava is best used in island cocktails.

TAMARIND *(Tamarindus indica)* Pod-like tamarind shells can be found among the large feathery trees around the BVI's. Some eat it straight up, directly from its brown shell, while others use it to create the most wonderful island sauces. Traditionalists will tell you to stew and preserve it, while those wishing to wet their whistle often steep the pulp in boiling water, add sugar, and chill before serving.

MANGO *(Mangifera indica)* Originally from Burma and Malaysia, local mangoes are just perfect, whether juiced, preserved, or served as ice-cream. Some even skewer pieces of the fruit and serve them on a kebab. Either way, you'll want to know how to cut a mango first and foremost. Start by cutting crosswise around either side of the pit. Next, score the flesh of the two pit-less portions, turning the unharmed skins inside out.

PAPAYA *(Carica papaya)* Also called pawpaw, Papaya is commonly used throughout the BVI's in drinks, salads, preserves, and, best of all, ice cream! Real kitchen experts also know that papaya leaves can serve as an excellent meat tenderizer. Those with an eye for gourmet offerings will often grill a wedge of papaya and serve with fresh fish.

Guavas on sale at an island fruit stand.

CHUTNEY DEFINED

Derived from the East Indian word chatni (meaning "strongly spiced"), chutney is now a worldwide condiment. Most chutney consists of a tasty mix of chopped fruits combined with spices, sugar, and vinegar, cooked into a slightly spicy spread. The sweet and tart flavor is often used to compliment strongly flavored meats, but is also used to perk up traditional crackers, toast, and bagels. There are thousands of possible combinations of ingredients for chutney and once you get the basic concept, any number of combinations await experimentation.

LOOKING FOR LOCAL GOODIES?

Swing by Dorothy's Superette on Main Street (Tortola), just past The Plaza. Dorothy provides the popular local rum, Callwood, as well as groceries and basic ingredients for many island recipes. Dorothy's Superette, 284-494-3757.

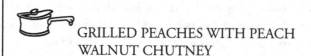

GRILLED PEACHES WITH PEACH WALNUT CHUTNEY

Ingredients:
Peach walnut chutney:
1 tbsp unsalted butter
½ cup diced onion
1 tbsp minced fresh ginger
¼ cup raisins
½ small tomato, peeled, seeded, and chopped
1 large peach, peeled and diced
½ cup vanilla syrup (reserved from poached peaches)
½ cup dry red wine
¼ cup balsamic vinegar
½ tsp salt
¼ cup coarsely chopped walnuts, toasted

Grilled Peaches:
2 cups water
2 cups sugar
½ vanilla bean, split lengthwise
1 cinnamon stick
2 whole cloves
1 whole allspice
4 ripe peaches, peeled, pitted and halved
4 ¼-inch-thick slices walnut bread
4 tbsp unsalted butter

LOCALS DO IT LIKE THIS:

Start by melting the butter in a skillet for the chutney. Add the ginger and onion, and continue to sauté for three minutes. Add the raisins, tomato, peach, vanilla syrup, red wine, vinegar, and salt. Do NOT add the walnuts. Bring this tasty mixture to a boil and then reduce, cooking on a low simmer for another twenty minutes while stirring frequently. When thick, add the walnuts and simmer for an additional five minutes. Cool and spoon into a container, reserving the chutney days in advance.

For the grilled peaches: Combine the water and sugar in a medium non-aluminum saucepan and bring to a boil over medium heat. Add the vanilla bean, cinnamon, cloves, and allspice and simmer for 15 minutes. Add the peach halves and continue to simmer for 3 to 10 minutes, or until the peach halves are tender; the amount of time will depend on the ripeness of the peaches. Remove the pan from heat and let the peaches cool in the syrup. Ten minutes before serving add the butter, sugar, vanilla bean, cinnamon stick, cloves, and allspice. Bring to a low boil. Next, rub the peach with the softened butter mixture and grill the peaches (cut side down) for approximately two minutes. Make sure to turn the peaches (very gently) and grill for an additional minute.

Optional: Grill bread on the side of the rack for thirty seconds, and serve as toast with the peaches and chutney.

Grilled Peaches—mmm, island good.

KINGS OF KIWI

The luxury charter yacht Madiba (Tel: +44 (0)1252 674878) is known for its exceptional cuisine (among other things), and fresh kiwi often find their way onto the plate of yachtsmen on board. Captain Dave van Reenen has built a reputation as a gracious host, but the real treat is found among Chef Glywnnis Wells' always stylish and seasonal menu. Ask Glywnnis about her signature dessert, Pavlova. A meringue-based treat, her winning recipe is served with fresh kiwi, fresh berries, and fresh whipped cream. Make sure to ask her about the story that goes along with the recipe.

LOOKING TO SPICE THINGS UP

Check out the Caribbean Corner Spice Shop on Main Street (Tortola), which boasts a well-stocked supply of herbs, spices, hot sauces, and some super-fine Cuban stogies. Caribbean Corner Spice Shop can be reached at 284-494-5564.

If you're still trying to heat things up, head over to the Sunny Caribbee Herb Spice Company, also on Main Street, for a famous selection of herbs and spices. Sunny Caribbee Herb Spice Company can be reached at 284-494-2178.

KIWIFRUIT CHUTNEY

Ingredients:
2 lbs kiwifruit
2 bananas
3 onions
3 lemons
1 cup brown sugar
1 tsp ground ginger
¼ tsp cayenne pepper
1 cup raisins
3 tbsp crystallized ginger
2 tsp salt
1 cup white vinegar

Locals Do It Like This:
Peel and slice the bananas and kiwi, chop the onions, and squeeze the lemon. Mix all ingredients and boil at low heat for one hour while stirring until thick. Cool and then spoon into a jar and seal.

HONEY-GINGER SAUCE

Ingredients:
1 (8-ounce) can sweetened tamarind nectar
1 tablespoon honey
Fresh ginger root (3 inches grated)
1 tablespoon soy sauce
1 tablespoon dry jerk seasoning
1 teaspoon cornstarch
1 teaspoon water

Locals Do It Like This:
Boil the honey and tamarind nectar. Gradually add the soy sauce, ginger, and dry jerk seasoning. Meanwhile, begin forming a paste by adding the cornstarch with the water, and then combining with the tamarind-honey mixture. Stir continuously until this tasty sauce thickens. Hot or cold, this fine recipe serves as a perfect dipping sauce or marinade for meats and local fish.

LEMON AND MUSTARD SEED CHUTNEY

Ingredients:
4 onions
5 lemons, seeded and chopped
1 oz salt
1 pint apple cider vinegar
1 oz mustard seeds
¼ lb raisins, seedless
A touch of allspice, ground
1 lb sugar
A touch of mace
2 cracked black peppercorns
A touch of cracked coriander

Locals Do It Like This:
Begin by sprinkling salt over the lemons and sliced onions. Let them sit for a minimum of twelve hours. Add the apple cider vinegar, mustard seeds, raisins, allspice, and sugar. Bring to a boil then simmer for 40 to 45 minutes. Cool and spoon into a jar and seal.

JERK SAUCE

Ingredients:
1 cup scallions (finely chopped)
1 onion (finely chopped)
2 teaspoons fresh thyme leaves
1 teaspoon salt
2 teaspoons sugar
1 teaspoon nutmeg (ground)
1 teaspoon Jamaican pimento (ground)
1 teaspoon cinnamon (ground)
1 Scotch bonnet (finely ground)
1 teaspoon black pepper (ground)
3 tablespoons soy sauce
1 tablespoon cider
1 tablespoon coconut oil

Locals Do It Like This:
Mix together all ingredients for a superb marinade for beef, chicken, and pork.

🔊 LOCAL TIP

Islanders like to use Lemon and Mustard Seed Chutney for beef, ham, and mutton.

🔊 LOCAL GARDENS

If you really want to soak in the flair of the islands, save some time to explore the J R O'Neal Botanic Garden, named after a famed BVI conservationist. First hatched as an agricultural research station, the site now serves as an eye-popping garden teeming with a hefty helping of species from BVI's natural habitats. With an emphasis on species unique to the region, visitors can take a gander at native plants brought into cultivation by the staff from the BVI National Parks Trust. Seek out the J R O'Neal Botanic Garden on Main Street on Tortola.

🔊 LOCAL PERSPECTIVE

"The preservation of pristine skies and seas, of unbleached coral reefs, and of unsoiled lands is not just a matter of public health or long-term conservation—it is a matter of immediate economic importance." —Former Chief Minister of the British Virgin Islands Hon. Dr. Orlando Smith

CHUTNEY CHATTER:

- Chutney is *not* relish: Typically chutneys are chunky and spreadable, much like a preserve. Relish is less sweet, crunchier, and rarely cooked.

- Chutney ingredients: Use firm-fleshed (under-ripe) fruits such as green apples, mangoes, bananas, peaches, and apricots. Consider rhubarb or under-ripe tomatoes as well. Soft fruits with delicate flavors do not work well, and their flavors are almost always lost. Dried fruits can work in chutneys but may add an overly tart flavor.

- The most common chutney spices and herbs are: cinnamon, ginger, cloves, nutmeg, allspice, cardamom, coriander, and mint.

- Adding onion and garlic is always a good choice.

- The most common chutney fruits are: apricot, raisin, mango, peach, tamarind, and citrus.

- Generally chutney is simply fruit, vinegar, and sugar cooked down to a reduction.

- In BVI, chutney is often eaten with fresh fish, using whatever local ingredients are seasonal at the time.

- Chutney is often blended with cream cheese, sour cream, or crème fraîche for spreads and fruit dip.

- To make a quick glaze for meat, add a touch of olive oil. To avoid charring when cooking meat, add the final glaze when the meat is almost done.

- When creating a marinade, before you glaze you'll want to boil your chutney again and then cool.

- Chutney will last for a few weeks in the refrigerator due to the acid and vinegar content. But if you want to preserve it, locals will tell you to can your chutney in a water bath (ten minutes in sterilized jars).

- The acid in chutney mixtures will often react with brass, iron, and copper pots, causing a metallic taste. Consider non-reactive pots instead. Wooden spoons are a good bet as well for the same reasons.

HOMETOWN HEROES

In the 1990s, a gaggle of concerned men and women began exploring ways to proactively protect BVI's marine environment. When charter yacht extraordinaire Trish Baily suggested a poster outlining steps for divers and boaters as a way to reduce damage to reefs, the loose-knit group began to spring into action. Soon a dedicated team formed, with members such as Alan and Eva Baskin, Clive Petrovic, Randy Keil, Chris and Kapua Gregory, Jane Bakewell, Clem Hill, and Roger Ellis. Also supporting the cause were a number of local organizations and businesses, such as the Tortola Ladies Club and TICO Wines and Spirits. With the success of such endeavors well under way, the group officially became the Association of Reef Keepers (ARK). As membership grew, this band of do-gooders continued to expand its educational outreach efforts to include briefing bareboat companies and crews on reef ecology, and distributing information to others that detailed the dangers of feeding fish. In addition, the ARK initiated the Erosion and Sedimentation Workshop and encouraged children to participate in environmental field days. As the organization prospered, their efforts were recognized on a worldwide scale, and further partnerships with marine environment organizations ensued. In 2005, the organization continued to transition and shape its cause as the ARK began directing much of its funds to the Island Resources Foundation, another organization dedicated to protecting the environment. With its sights set on the impact of major development projects on small islands, the ARK's mission has since fit nicely with the goals of the Island Resources Foundation. As a combined force, the organizations have now distributed information throughout all of the Caribbean.

Among its many achievements, the ARK has developed simple—yet effective—guidelines, some of which can be found below:

> **DIVERS**
> **SNORKELLERS BOATERS**
> **The coral reefs are precious and delicate.**
> **Their future depends on you.**
> Worldwide coral reefs are suffering degradation from various fac-tors—pollution, overfishing,
> excess nutrients
> … and tourist activity.
>
> PLEASE TAKE CARE NOT TO INFLICT FURTHER DAMAGE.

TOUCH NOTHING

The slightest touch with hands, fins or equipment can irreparably damage coral polyps, the tiny animals that build the coral reefs. Remember, most corals only grow a half inch per year.

REMAIN HORIZONTAL

Remain horizontal in the water and snorkel in water over your depth. Snorkeling on shallow reefs can easily inflict damage to the coral and cause personal injury. In a vertical position, your flapping fins are killers! They break coral and stir up sediment that can smother the coral polyps. For equipment adjustment, swim out and away from the coral into deep water.

POMEGRANATE TREES

Head to Katitche Point Greathouse (www.katitche.com) for a gander at the pomegranate tree gracing the courtyard that connects the whimsical bedrooms. Katitche Point Greathouse, built by renowned British architect Michael Helm, whose designs are regularly featured in Architectural Digest magazine, is a true masterpiece. The vacation villas offered at Katitche Point, hovering above Virgin Gorda's spectacular Mahoe Bay, are home to a number of lime trees, olive trees, and pomegranate trees—perfect for your next recipe.

MANGO TREES

Mangoes, the king of fruits, are found in abundance on the rugged southern coast of Tortola. Mango trees typically produce fruit approximately five years after planting and bear fruit for forty years, with trees producing an average of one hundred mangoes each year. Just before the fruit is formed, the tree is decorated with tiny, pinkish white flower blossoms. Popular due to their exotic sweetness, mangoes are also known for their nutritional value. For example, mangoes contain an enzyme that serves as a soothing digestive aid, stimulates metabolism, and purifies the intestinal tract. Mangoes are also a powerful antioxidant and in many countries used as blood builders due to their high iron content. In addition, mangoes, which have a high potassium and magnesium content, are perfect for stress, muscle cramps, and heart problems.

POMEGRANATE CHUTNEY

Ingredients:
½ cup red currant jelly
⅓ cup finely chopped green onions, including tops
1 tbsp minced fresh jalapeno chili
½ tsp ground coriander
1 cup pomegranate seeds (generally takes 1 lb of pomegranate)
1 tbsp minced fresh ginger
1 tbsp lemon juice
A touch of salt and pepper

Locals Do It Like This:
Begin a day early! Start by removing pomegranate seeds a day ahead, and make sure to chill overnight in an airtight container. On the following day, 20 minutes before serving, heat currant jelly for approximately 10-20 seconds in a microwave to soften. Next, stir in the pomegranate seeds, ginger, chili, onions, lemon juice, salt, pepper, and coriander. Let stand for approximately 20 minutes before serving.

CARIBBEAN MANGO SAUCE

Ingredients:
1 cup fresh mango (diced)
2 tablespoons pineapple (crushed)
2 teaspoons fine granulated sugar
⅛ teaspoon coconut milk

Locals Do It Like This:
Combine the diced mango, crushed pineapple, sugar, and coconut milk together into a bowl. Use a food processor or blender to mix the ingredients until the mixture is smooth. Spoon the sauce into a container and refrigerate. This island favorite is perfect for everything from grilled chicken and fish (such as snapper) to waffles and desserts.

APPLE AND GREEN TOMATO CHUTNEY

Ingredients:
2 lbs green tomatoes
2 lbs tart apples
½ lb onions
1 lb raisins
3 ¾ cups light brown sugar
2 tsp ground ginger
2 tsp black peppercorns, crushed
A touch of nutmeg, grated
2 tbsp coarse salt
2 garlic cloves
3 cups wine vinegar

Locals Do It Like This:
Chop the green tomatoes, peel and chop the apples, and chop the onions. Combine green tomatoes, apples, onions, raisins, brown sugar, ginger, black peppercorns, nutmeg, salt, and cloves. Do NOT include the vinegar. Stir all ingredients and bring to a boil. Cook over low heat while gradually adding the vinegar. Stir for approximately 45 minutes as the mixture thickens. Remove from heat, cool, and seal in a container.

TROPICAL MANGO SALSA

Ingredients:
1 ripe mango (peeled, pitted, and diced)
½ medium red onion (finely chopped)
1 Scotch bonnet (stemmed, seeded and minced)
1 cucumber (peeled and diced)
1 red bell pepper (diced)
3 tablespoons fresh cilantro leaves (chopped)
3 tablespoons fresh lime juice
Salt
Pepper

Locals Do It Like This:
Combine all of the ingredients in a bowl, and salt and pepper to taste. Perfect for grilled fish.

LOOKING FOR THE PERFECT APPLE?

Try the BVI sugar apple (Annona squamosa), known as the sweetsop or custard apple! From drinks to chutneys, the sugar apple is always a tasty addition to any recipe.

ENJOYING THE PERFECT MANGO

Once you've located the perfect mango, apply the squeeze technique to make sure it is soft and ready to eat. When fully ripened, you'll note an exotic perfume-like fragrance. Mangoes can be enjoyed raw (just be prepared, they are juicy) by simply peeling back the skin and eating it like a banana. To cut the mango, stand the fruit on its stem end and slice downwards alongside the seed. Repeat on the other side, and then scoop out the flesh with a spoon (or you can cube the mango by cutting crosshatch lines partway through the flesh). Mangoes can be added to smoothies, sauces, salads, sorbets, and soups.

THE BEST LOCAL CHUTNEY:

- ◇ Roti Palace (284-494-4196): Their mango chutney is a classic.
- ◇ Pam's Kitchen (284-495-9237): Call Pam and ask her to dingy directly to your boat.
- ◇ Sunny Caribbee (284-494-2178): Try the papaya chutney.
- ◇ Tradewinds (284-770-476-9988): A tasty banana chutney awaits.
- ◇ Bananakeet Cafe (284-494-5842): With some of the best BVI sunsets around, the Bananakeet, located between Cane Garden and Carrot Bay on Tortola, boasts a killer mango and pineapple chutney.
- ◇ Hawks Nest Management (284-495-1677): This property management company, owned by Albert Stoutt and Donna Arter, not only links vacationers up with snazzy digs, they also offer private chef services. Mixed among their culinary offerings, the Hawks Nest dishes some tasty chutney, often served with a tropical style curried chicken, yogurt sauce, diced mango, bananas, and coconut shavings.
- ◇ *William Thornton*, also called Willy T (284-496-8603/VHF Channels 16 or 74): Try their version of mango chutney and you won't want to leave this floating restaurant anchored in the Bight on Norman Island.
- ◇ The Fat Virgin's Café (284-495-7052): This casual waterside café, located at Biras Creek Resort's dock, is home to some of the best homemade chutney in BVI. Also, try their famous outdoor-grilled burger in paradise while chutney hopping.

PEAR CHUTNEY

Ingredients:
3 lbs fresh pears, unpeeled, cored, and diced
1 lb brown sugar
2 cups cider vinegar
1 onion, chopped
1 cup golden raisins
¼ cup diced, preserved ginger
1 clove garlic, minced
½ tsp cayenne pepper
2 tsp salt
½ tsp cinnamon
½ tsp cloves
2 tsp mustard seed

Locals Do It Like This:
Core and dice the fresh pears, but do not peel. Combine the brown sugar and vinegar in a saucepan and bring to a boil. Next, add the pears and all remaining ingredients. Cook slowly, while stirring, for one hour. Cool and scoop into a jar and seal.

GRILLED RED PEPPER CHUTNEY

Ingredients:
3 red bell peppers
2 green onions
2 tbsp olive oil
⅛ tsp cumin seeds
⅛ tsp caraway seeds
⅛ tsp coriander seeds
1 tbsp minced fresh cilantro
1 tbsp sherry wine vinegar
Salt, freshly ground black pepper, and cayenne pepper to taste

Locals Do It Like This:
Use the olive oil to coat the chopped red peppers and green onions. Grill the peppers and onions, turning frequently, until the onions turn bright green and the peppers blister. Remove the peppers from the grill and place in a mixing bowl. Let stand for ten minutes before removing the seeds and skin from the peppers. Cut the grilled onions into 1-inch lengths, and then chop both the peppers and onions. Combine the cumin, coriander, and caraway in a sauté pan and toast over low heat for approximately 2 minutes. Let cool for one minute and then use a food processor or a mortar and pestle to create a fine powder. When finished, add this to the pepper and onion mixture and add the cilantro, vinegar, salt, pepper, and cayenne.

◇ DID YOU KNOW?

Chutney is also music! Indigenous to the southern Caribbean, chutney music is up-tempo and is played in rhythms imported from calypso, reggae, and soca. Created from a hodge-podge of influences, early chutney was religious and most often performed by Trinidadian female members before a wedding celebration. When Sundar Popo hit the charts in 1970 with "Nana and Nani," chutney began to enjoy mainstream success. Typically chutney lyrics are written in Hindi, Bhojpuri, or English. Head to one of the many carnivals (BVI Music Festival in May, BVI Emancipation Festival in August, or BVI Spring Regatta and Sailing Festival), and you'll get a taste of a variety of Caribbean music.

◇ FERRY SUGGESTIONS

If you're chutney hopping in search of the best chutney eats in BVI you'll need to know the ferry schedule. Try these reliable rides below:
◇ Speedy's, 284-495-5240
◇ Smith's Ferry Service, 284-495-4495
◇ North Sound Express, 284-495-2271
◇ Native Son Inc., 284-495-4617
◇ David Straker, private charter, 284-495-6168
◇ St. Thomas Ferry (from Tortola), 809-775-6501
◇ St. John Ferry (from Tortola/West End), 284-495-4166
◇ Saba Rock Ferry (from Virgin Gorda/Gun Creek), 284-495-7711
◇ Nubian Princess, 284-495-4999
◇ Jost Van Dyke Ferry Service, 284-495-9278
◇ Peter Island Ferry (from Tortola), 284-495-2000
◇ Marina Cay Ferry (from Beef Island), 284-494-2174
◇ North Sound Power Boat Services, 284-495-7612

SCOTCH BONNET

The humble little Scotch bonnet is at the center of one of the hottest cooking trends today. Its power is routinely touted in *Chili Pepper* magazine, and celebrity chefs, like Allan Susser and Stephen Raichlen, now feature this as their favorite pepper.

Often oblivious to the rest of the world's newfound fascination with Scotch bonnet, BVIslanders know that their pepper is the hottest on the planet—packing the heat of fifty jalapeños or more. It is so popular on the islands that pepper almost always means Scotch bonnet!

This small but popular chili is easily recognized by its wooly cap and multiple colors. If you want to eat like a local, ask for the hidden jar full of vinegar and peppers behind the counter. Whereas some tourists may dump Tabasco on their stew or oxtail, a real islander always opts for the savory Scotch bonnet.

Considered by many to be the soul of the Caribbean, the use of these chilis is a result of the Arawak and Carib Indians, expert pepper-sauce makers. Before salt was used to flavor fish, these tribes mixed up a tasty brew of coui, a hot pepper and cassava juice concoction. Since that time BVIslanders have been seasoning their foods with hot peppers. Islanders know that these peppers are also good for you, as they are rich in vitamin E and are popular among home remedies that cure everything from the common flu to arthritis.

Many cooks discovered early on that Scotch bonnet combined with thyme, onions, and coconut milk was one heck of a seasoning for local fish. Most local chefs have their own pepper tree, and no family table is without a small dish of sliced Scotch bonnet or a jar of pepper sauce. Some chefs add vinegar, carrots, allspice berries, cho-cho slices, and garlic to their tableside sauces as well.

Don't be surprised if you even find a splash of Scotch bonnet sauce in freshly squeezed orange juice too; it'll start your day off right!

To do it the BVI way, add a Scotch bonnet to your recipes.

PICK-A-PEPPER TIP:

If you want to make the greatest impact, you'll need to snag a whole Scotch bonnet and mince it (including its membrane and seeds). Go easy at first, introducing a very small amount to any recipe! For a milder version, opt for "mutton pepper" which is a hybrid variety of Scotch bonnet that lacks the over-the-top flame of the common pepper. Another way to reduce pepper heat is to remove the seeds and membranes (known as veins).

Don't worry, you're not a sissy if you use rubber gloves: these suckers are hot and you want to make sure they never touch your eyes, or nose.

Can it really be that Hot?

You bet! Consider this; the Scoville scale is a measure of the "hotness," or piquancy, of a chili pepper. Most Scotch bonnets have a heat rating that rings in at 200,000-325,000 Scoville Units. To put this into context, its habanero cousin typically tops out at a little over 200,000. While this puppy is not to be missed when sampling BVI cuisine, it should be noted that eating whole, raw Scotch bonnet peppers is not advised for those unaccustomed to munching on super spicy food.

Can't Take the Heat Tip:

If you get an overdose, grab a glass of milk or any dairy product. Starchy foods will also absorb the capsaicin.

Habanera vs. Scotch Bonnet:

The red *Capsicum chinense* pods are Scotch bonnet, while habanera are usually orange and are lantern shaped.

Scotch Bonnet Not Hot Enough? Try This …

Surprisingly, neither the Scotch bonnet nor the habanero is the hottest pepper. If you want to test the hottest you'll have to seek out the bird pepper, a wild form of Capsicum annuum. Bird peppers are not found near the BVI but are often collected in the mountains of northern Mexico where locals call them chili depajaro. Interestingly, birds cannot taste the hotness of peppers, which has led farmers in some parts of the world to feed their turkeys hot peppers in order to flavor their flesh so they become distasteful to carnivores.

If you really want to get to know the islands, check out some of the fun facts and projects offered by the Jost Van Dykes Preservation Society (JVDPS), a not-for-profit dedicated to the preservation of BVI culture through conservation, cultivation, education, and research. Serving as a microcosm of the rich history and beauty of BVI as a whole, Jost Van Dyke is only lightly developed (electricity arrived in 1992) and has approximately 250 residents. Most of the land on this beautiful island belongs to BVI citizens and their families, with local laws protecting it from outside investment. JVDPS endeavors to protect key elements of this culture for future generations to enjoy its white sands, untouched hillsides, floral beauty, and unbelievable wildlife. JVDPS projects include the construction of a modern island wooden sloop to honor the island's maritime heritage and to serve as an educational platform for building and sailing. This passionate group routinely seeks volunteers and sponsors, while partnering with others such as the BVI government, H.L. Stoutt College Marine Studies Program, the BVI National Parks and Trusts, and the Trustees of the BVI National Parks.

⚓ ISLAND OBSERVATIONS
"The wonderful people of the BVI understand that they live in a unique environment worth protecting. We all know that the national parks need constant attention. They are being managed for the next generation and the next."—Peter Jennings

MARGARITA SALSA

Ingredients:
3 tbsp fine tequila
½ cup onion, chopped
2 cups fresh mango, diced
1 ½ Scotch bonnet, seeded and minced
2 tbsp fresh cilantro, chopped
1 tsp lime peel, grated
2 tbsp fresh lime juice
¼ tsp cumin, ground

Locals Do It Like This:
Blend the tequila, onion, mango, Scotch bonnet, fresh cilantro, lime peel, lime juice, and cumin. Serve at room temperature with grilled shrimp, chicken, or pork.

AVOCADO AND KIWI SALSA

Ingredients:
1½ cup kiwi (diced)
2 ripe avocados (diced)
⅓ cup fresh cilantro (chopped)
2 scallions (thinly sliced)
1 Scotch bonnet (chopped)
1 tablespoon lime juice
Salt to taste

Locals Do It Like This:
Mix all of the ingredients in a bowl. Add the avocado last, making sure to toss gently. Serve immediately.

TEN REASONS TO SUPPORT BVI FARMERS

By supporting local BVI farmers you are supporting the entire movement toward sustainability. In other words, you are encouraging BVI as a whole to honor, celebrate, and protect its own unique food traditions. Instead of moving toward the corporate globalization of the food economy, you are encouraging BVI to keep its own healthy food traditions intact to further support the livelihood of the local community, as well as protect the health of those within the community.

◇ When you seek out and support local agriculture, you are simultaneously supporting local culture, and in turn, further celebrating diversity within the local BVI farming community.

◇ By supporting local farmers and merchants you support not only the local farming community, but the local economy as well.

◇ By purchasing food directly from farmers, you ensure that they earn a fair and adequate pay for their quality goods. The best way of supporting local BVI farmers is to buy local produce directly from the grower at a farmer's market or roadside stand, many of which offer cheaper fruit and vegetables than supermarkets. It is also equally important to support local independent shops.

◇ When you buy and eat locally-grown food you are more likely to avoid the risks of genetically altered foods that dominate the global marketplace. For example, most transgenic crops are grown on large factory-style farms and as a result often trigger allergies and pose environmental risks.

◇ By supporting local farmers you support the land and open spaces held in place by farmers. Instead of being snatched up and developed into large hotels, local farmers keep the landscape from becoming altered and they keep the landscape rural.

◇ When you support local farmers, you develop awareness among children of the importance of farming cultures and the rural landscapes that surround the local community. Whether local or tourist, by bringing children to a farmer's market, you teach and maintain the tradition of farming. Purchasing directly from farmers allows tikes to learn how their produce is grown, harvested, sold, and best enjoyed. As a result, children gain a sense of future responsibility for respecting surrounding farming communities in BVI or at home.

◇ By supporting local farmers and buying locally produced food, you gain a better understanding of how seasonally grown food adapts to the climate.

◇ When you support a local farmer, you support yourself; as the fresh foods produced by local farmers are always better for you than the vitamin-depleted produce you receive from larger supermarkets, some of which receive their food after days of transportation, repackaging, and trimming.

◇ By seeking out and supporting local farmers, you not only receive fresh and nutritious foods, but you also get such goodies at wholesale prices without the hike in price applied by a middleman.

◇ When you support local farmers, you effectively reduce fossil fuel use and carbon emissions.

RANDOM ISLAND TIDBITS

- If you're looking for all-organic, fresh local chicken and eggs then give Trevor Bishop a ring for handy home delivery. (284-495-7300 or 284-495-7585)

- If you're wondering about the water—wonder no longer, it's desalinated saltwater and of drinking quality. Water is a valuable commodity, so use it sparingly!

- If you're looking for a night out on the town to explore good eats and treats, sans children, then consider Tropical Nannies, a qualified childcare service available for vacationers staying at a resort, rental villa, or home. (284-495-6493 or www. tropicalnannies.com)

- If you're looking for family fun, check out the Fireball Full Moon Party at Trellis Bay Cyber Café on Beef Island. Starting at 7 PM, West Indian BBQ is served along with live fungi music, Mocko Jumbies, fire-juggling, and Aragorn-Dick Read's famous fireball sculptures.

- If you're in the mood for a little gaming fun, try the Humane Society's Gaming Night, one of the biggest fundraisers for BVI animal lovers. The event boasts more than five hundred prizes, including lunches and dinners at some of BVI's best restaurants and hotels. Locals and vacationers alike enjoy blackjack, poker, roulette, and the hometown favorite—crab races.

- If you're in search of exotic spices and homemade goodies, head to St. William's Catholic Church for their "Hurry, Hurry Come for the Curry" night. The large dining room is filled with unbeatable curries along with other sweet and savory condiments and homemade desserts.

 MANGO FRUIT SPREAD

Ingredients:
3 cups one-inch mango chunks
2 cups one-inch pineapple chunks
2 tablespoons lemon zest
1 package fruit pectin for light jam
2 teaspoons ground cinnamon
1 teaspoon ground cloves
Honey

Locals Do It Like This:
Mix all ingredients in a saucepan over medium heat, stirring frequently. Remove the spread from heat and pour into a sterilized container. Let cool at room temperature for twenty-four hours and then refrigerate.

GUAVA SALSA

Ingredients:
2 tomatoes (chopped)
½ guava (chopped)
1 garlic clove (chopped)
1 bunch parsley (chopped)

Locals Do It Like This:
Simply mix these fresh ingredients together and enjoy. Guava salsa is unforgettable when served over pan-fried grouper.

CHUTNEY WITH MINT

Ingredients:
1 lb tart apples
1 lb tomatoes
2 cups sugar
3 sweet peppers
10 small onions
½ cup fresh mint leaves, chopped
1 ⅓ cup seeded raisins
3 cups vinegar
2 tsp dry mustard
1 tsp salt

Locals Do It Like This:
Peel the tomatoes; chop the veggies and the fruit. Add the marvelous mint. Scald and cool vinegar. Next add mustard, salt, and sugar—and combine with all chopped ingredients. Mix, mix, mix. Cover and refrigerate.

COCONUT-MINT SAUCE

Ingredients:
¼ cup toasted coconut (shredded/flaked)
1 teaspoon minced ginger
1 clove garlic
2 tablespoons mint leaves (chopped)
¼ cup vegetable broth
2 tablespoons agave nectar
1 teaspoon soy sauce
1 tablespoon lemon juice

Locals Do It Like This:
Mix all tasty ingredients together and puree in a blender until smooth.

☧ OTHER MARVELOUS MINT CREATIONS

Take a crack at the chocolate bourbon mint cake at Chez Bamboo (284-495-5752), or better yet try your hand at the flourless chocolate torte with raspberry coulis and fresh mint prepared by Blue Iguana Catering, one of the top choice caterers with an excellent reputation for gourmet food (they cater the Royal British Virgin Islands Yacht Club). Try 284-494-5306 or e-mail enquiries@bviweddings.com. And, not to be outdone in the world of all things mint, the chef on the Motor Yacht La Buscadora offers up a tasty Butterfield, New Zealand leg of lamb with a dijon herb crust complimented by a mint and onion sauce served with pommes Anna and a vegetable medley. Give them a ring at 284-494-6017 or mail@bvicrewedyachts.com.

TAMARIND CLUB

What better place for a chance at authentic tamarind chutney than at the actual Tamarind Club. Nestled in the valley of Josiah's Bay, this hidden oasis offers a swim-up bar, tropical gardens, and, of course, lots of fresh local ingredients. Tamarind takes center stage as guests at the unique inn dine on rack of lamb with tamarind chutney, tamarind chicken breast stuffed with crab, and the ever-so-popular Sunday brunch with a wide selection of entrees, including tamarind BBQ ribs and chicken. Give them a shout at 284-495-2477 or visit their Web site at www.tamarindclub.com.

TAMARIND CHUTNEY

Ingredients:
1 tbsp canola oil
1 tsp cumin seeds
1 tsp ground ginger
½ tsp cayenne pepper
½ tsp fennel seeds
½ tsp asafoetida powder
½ tsp garam masala
2 cups water
1⅛ cups white sugar
3 tbsp tamarind paste

Locals Do It Like This:
Begin by heating the canola oil in a pan over low to medium heat. Add the cumin seeds, ginger, cayenne pepper, fennel, asafoetida, and garam masala. Cook all ingredients, stirring for three minutes. Next, add the water into the pan with the spices along with the sugar and tamarind paste. Bring to a boil. Reduce heat and simmer for approximately 30 minutes.

 TAMARIND SAUCE

Ingredients:
¼ cup tamarind pulp
1¼ cups water
1 tablespoon raw sugar
¼ teaspoon black pepper
½ teaspoon chili powder
½ teaspoon cumin seeds (ground)
1 tablespoon fresh mint leaves (chopped)

Locals Do It Like This:
Start by soaking the tamarind pulp in water the night before preparing this tasty sauce. After twenty-four hours, mash the tamarind pulp in the water and blend. Next, strain the liquid through cheesecloth. Begin combining all remaining ingredients, with the exception of the mint, and whisk. Chill and add the mint just before serving.

BEST RESTAURANT AWARDS

And the winners are ...

- **|●|** Best Place for Caribbean fusion: The Bananakeet Café at the Heritage Inn in Windy Hill (284-494-5842; www.heritageinnbvi.com/restaurant.shtml). There are many reasons to go, and at the top of that list has to be either the banana leaf fish of the night or the honey mint rack of lamb found at this Tortola dining destination!
- **|●|** Best Place for Caribbean-style BBQ: Jolly Roger at Soper's Hole in West End, Tortola, (284-495-4599). Pop in and ask Louis to cook up some of his famous BVI creations. Low-key and very knowledgeable about all things BVI, Louis will show you what Caribbean-style BBQ is all about. His hundred foot dock is also a great spot to dingy up for a quick bite!
- **|●|** Best Place for Bresaola (slices of cured beef): Capriccio di Mare, Road Town, Tortola (284-494-5369). This picture-perfect Italian café offers not only the best bresaola, but also some of the best pizza on the island (they top their pies with grilled eggplant). Don't forget to also try their signature mango bellini.
- **|●|** Best Place for Mango Salsa: Chillin' Café, Road Town, Tortola (284-494-9236). Though Chillin' has a wide variety of fusion cuisine and a strong wine list, the real winner at this eatery is the mango salsa, a tasty side that the chef often adds to a hefty West Indian crab cake dish.
- **|●|** Best Place for Doved Pork: Netty's Diner (284-495-9001), located on a dead-end street behind Stanley's on Tortola, is a hidden gem. Netty and her daughter Janelle are known for the best doved pork, browned and then cooked in a secret sauce, on the island.
- **|●|** Best Calamari Ceviche: *William Thornton* (284-496-8603), better known as Willy T, dishes calamari seasoned with Asian herbs and spices served on a bed of fresh lettuce, tomato, cucumber, and a secret ginger-soy vinaigrette.

Courtesy of William Thornton.

Willy T—fun, food, and sun are found at this floating restaurant.

CRAZY OVER COCONUT

BVI legend Mrs. Scatliffe knows coconut. In fact, this Tortola institution serves a famous chicken and coconut entrée that is boiled with carrot, onion, and celery, thickening the resulting broth with flour. The secret ingredient to this thickening method however is the coconut milk, which is really coconut meat that is soaked in water and then squeezed through cheesecloth. To top it off, Mrs. Scatliffe serves the popular dish in a coconut shell, and then presents it by candlelight on an open air terrace.

HOW TO CRACK A COCONUT

There are certainly many ways to open a coconut, from banging on it with a hammer to poking holes in the eyes to drain the liquid before having at it. No matter how you cut it, the outer shell is quite thick and hard, creating a challenge for the average famished tourist. Experts know the trick is to hold your beloved coconut over a bowl and give it several solid whacks with the blunt side (back) of a cleaver. Focus on the center of the coconut until it cracks open cleanly into equal halves. Make sure to catch the juice in the bowl as it drains. If it's fresh, enjoy the juice by itself, mmmm, or save it for your favorite recipe.

 COCONUT CHUTNEY

Ingredients:
2 cups of fresh coconut, shredded
10 dry red chilies
1 sprig curry leaf
A dash of asoefetida (optional)
½ tsp methi (fenugreek) seeds
2 tsp udad dhal
2 tsp channa dhal
1 tomato

Locals Do It Like This:
Heat oil in a sauté pan and add the curry leaves, asoefetida, methi seeds, and dhal. Add the coconut and chopped tomatoes and blend all ingredients into a paste. Serve over rice.

 PAPAYA-COCONUT JAM

Ingredients:
2 cups fresh coconut (grated)
4 cups papayas (pureed)
4 cups sugar
1 box dry fruit pectin
¼ cup lemon juice
1 tablespoon fresh ginger (grated)

Locals Do It Like This:
Combine and cook the grated coconut, papaya puree, sugar, and box of dry pectin for fifteen minutes. Add the lemon juice and the fresh ginger for an additional five minutes. Pour into sterilized containers.

RED ONION CHUTNEY

Ingredients:
1 bunch fresh cilantro
4 green chilis (fresh jalapenos or Scotch bonnet)
1 red onion, chopped
1 tbsp fresh ginger, chopped
¼ cup fresh mint leaves
1 tsp sugar
3 tbsp lemon juice
A dash of salt

Locals Do It Like This:
Cut the stems from the cilantro and discard. Mix all ingredients in a food processor or use a mortar and pestle, until smooth. Serve fresh.

 PINEAPPLE PLANTAIN CHUTNEY

Ingredients:
2 tablespoons butter
1 plantain (peeled and chopped)
2 cups fresh pineapple (peeled and chopped)
½ cup of dry white wine
½ cup chicken stock
½ Scotch bonnet (seeded and minced)

Locals Do It Like This:
Melt the butter over medium heat while adding the plantain. Sauté for five minutes until golden in color. Remove the plantain from heat and begin to mix in all other ingredients. Return to medium heat and stir for ten minutes. Add the plantain back to the mixture and stir to blend. This tasty chutney is perfect for grilled local fish.

MAKE IT WITH MANGO

Red onion chutney is stellar as a stand-alone dish, but toss in some mango and it's unbeatable. Red onion and mango chutney is made in practically the same fashion; just stir in four peeled and cut mangoes and pineapple juice to amp up this chutney creation.

NATURE'S INGREDIENTS

Many of the best island recipes are inspired by the lush and tropical gardens that blanket BVI. For a real understanding of how the natural surroundings influence everything from BVI cooking to BVI culture, make sure to explore the many national parks (many are accessible only by boat). Here are just a few of the many worth a visit:

Cam Bay National Park: Located on Great Camanoe, Cam Bay boasts a salt pond, migratory wading birds, and endless tropical flora.

Diamond Cay: Located on Jost Van Dyke, this idyllic destination is lined with beaches, cliffs, pelicans, leatherback turtles, and a vibrant reef.

Gorda Peak: Located on Virgin Gorda, this 265-acre national park is home to the island's highest point of 1,370 feet. Explore this park for an endless variety of indigenous exotic plants and mahogany trees.

Prickly Pear National Park: Located on Prickly Pear Island, this 243-acre oasis boasts cacti-covered hills, white, black, and red mangroves, four salt ponds, and tamarind trees.

A DAY OF SNORKELING (AND CHUTNEY TASTING)

Head to Myett's on Cane Garden Bay and snorkel at Smuggler's Cove. On your way back from Smuggler's Cove, check out the beach at the Long Bay Resort; it's absolutely amazing. Start your day with a hearty breakfast on the deck at the 1841 House at Long Bay (ask if there is any fresh chutney). You'll certainly enjoy their seaside goodies on a deck overlooking the bay. Next, head to the beach and explore Long Bay, leaving plenty of time for lounging and relaxing. When you've soaked in the sights, head over to Smuggler's Cove (it's about a ten minute drive) and dip in for more snorkeling adventures. As the day winds down, hit Myett's at Cane Garden Bay for a late afternoon happy hour and dinner.

BVI QUOTES

"Land and ocean are inextricably linked together. Parks are the symbol of this relationship. The economic success of small ocean nations such as the British Virgin Islands is dependent upon the sustainable management of its parks."— Jean-Michel Cousteau

 AVOCADO TOMATO SALSA

Ingredients:
2 avocados
1 tomato
⅓ cup onion, minced
1 lime, juiced
1 tsp Scotch bonnet sauce
2 tsp Carib beer
1 ½ tsp oil
⅓ cup green onion, minced
2 tsp ginger, minced

Locals Do It Like This:
Mix all ingredients together and enjoy. Refrigerate for one hour before serving.

 BANANA SALSA

Ingredients:
2 bananas
½ cup green bell pepper, diced
½ cup red bell pepper, diced
1 Scotch bonnet pepper
1 tbsp ginger, minced
3 scallions, chopped
¼ cup cilantro leaves, chopped
3 tbsp lime juice
2 tbsp light brown sugar
¼ tsp ground cardamom
2 tbsp olive oil
Salt and pepper

Locals Do It Like This:
Mix all of these sweet-tasting ingredients together, adding salt, pepper, and lime juice to taste. Cover and refrigerate until serving.

PINEAPPLE, MANGO, AND CUCUMBER SALSA

Ingredients:
½ cup pineapple, diced
½ cup mango
½ cup cucumber, diced
⅓ cup red bell pepper, diced
⅓ tomato, diced
3 tbsp green onion, chopped
1 tbsp mint
2 limes, juiced
Scotch bonnet pepper (optional)
Salt

Locals Do It Like This:
Cut and dice all ingredients, mixing together and seasoning to taste. Chill and serve with fish.

BVI TROPICAL FRUIT SALSA

Ingredients:
1 mango, peeled, pitted, and chopped
1 papaya, chopped
1 avocado, chopped
3 tbsp lime juice
2 tbsp fresh cilantro, chopped
2 tbsp brown sugar
1 tsp Scotch bonnet pepper
1 tsp ginger, crushed

Locals Do It Like This:
Combine all ingredients, mixing together. Refrigerate for at least one hour. Serve with fresh local fish or chicken.

COCONUT SHRIMP AND TROPICAL SALSA

Don't be fooled, salsa is not just for tortilla chips. If the tropical variety strikes your fancy, make sure to try it with golden brown shrimp. Locals do it best when they dredge the fresh shrimp in a Carib beer batter, and then coat them with fresh shredded coconut before placing in hot oil. They serve this tasty coconut shrimp and tropical salsa with fried plantains and a cold beer.

ISLAND LINGO

As a friendly gesture, always opt for a cheery "Good Morning," "Good Afternoon," or "Good Night."

If you're headed south, you "go down island." If you're headed north, you "go up island."

If you need an automatic when renting a car, ask for a "mash'n'go."

When the power goes off, it's often referred to as "da current."

Flip-flops and sandals are often known as "slippers."

When you're ready to relax and party, use "We be limin' mon."

Chapter Four

Drink Up

BARS OF BVI

The British Virgin Islands, within sight of the U.S. Virgin Islands, may lack the hustle and bustle of the mainland but makes up for it with distinct and hidden gems. You just have to know where to find them.

Peering at the Caribbean on a world map, it's a bit difficult to distinguish between the fifty or so islands and cays that make up the British Virgin Islands. About ninety miles east of Puerto Rico and northeast of the U.S. Virgin Islands, your best bet is to find your information the old fashioned way: just ask a bartender.

Edith, the bartender at Mad Dog's, is a good start. Crack open a Carib, the legendary island pilsner, and ask this hometown hero to share her tropical secrets. Her pub, serving as the quintessential beach bar, is perched on the rocks just above an outcropping of seaside boulders on Virgin Gorda. Known throughout the BVI, and perhaps even the world, as the creator of the best Pina Coladas, Edith will certainly dish out the island lowdown. With her quiet and unassuming way, she politely declines to answer questions related to her secret cocktail ingredients, but will happily point adventure-seekers to the best kept secrets of the British Virgin Islands.

For instance, Jost Van Dyke, a four mile long island nearby, is known as the "barefoot island" due to its casual lifestyle. However, local bartenders will warn you not to let the nickname fool you. Jost Van Dyke may be a favorite destination of yachties and movie stars, due to its protected anchorages and relatively unknown status, but it is still one of the best party islands of the Caribbean.

Foxy Callwood is to be credited for the hoopla, as this larger-than-life bartender/owner has hosted some of the biggest parties on the island at his popular beachside watering hole. Known simply as Foxy's, this destination has hosted Halloween parties, catamaran races, and legendary New Year's Eve parties to name just a few. At one time, such antics were enjoyed only by those lucky enough to stumble upon this hidden beach bar while boating or cruising in their twenty-six million dollar mega-yachts. Today, a mixture of tourists, Rastafarians, European backpackers, and locals converge on this tiny island along with a famous face or two. At times, boats in the harbor are so plentiful it's common to see vacationers hop from watercraft to watercraft (and be offered a beer along the way) just to make it to the sandy spit of beach.

Every good bartender in the BVI will tell you that before leaving Jost Van Dyke you must try a "Painkiller" (a mighty rum concoction) invented at the Soggy Dollar Bar. Named "Best Beach Bar in the Caribbean" in 2000 and 2001, it didn't come as a surprise that Islands magazine chose the dig as "The Number One Watering Hole in the World" in 2002. Despite its fame, the Soggy Dollar Bar has no dock, often leaving thirsty patrons to swim ashore from their boat, thus paying for drinks with "soggy dollars." If you're brave, or intoxicated, dare to invite the bartender Kendrick (call him KC) to a game of ring-toss before you leave.

Just down the Sir Francis Drake Passage is another treasure—Treasure Island that is. In actuality, it's called Norman Island, the acclaimed island on which the Robert Louis Stevenson's Treasure Island was based. After the brig called William Thornton sunk, locals resurrected what is now known as Willy T, a world famous floating restaurant. Leave your worries behind, and start limin'. This floating party on the sea is family friendly by day and popular for partygoers by night. Lunch and dinner are not to be missed, but it's the tropical cocktails found on the Willy T that are all the rage.

Despite a sleepier image, the British Virgin Islands have left their stamp on the Caribbean; just ask a local bartender.

PAINKILLER

Ingredients:
2 oz dark rum
1 oz cream of coconut
1 oz orange juice
4 oz pineapple juice

Locals Do It Like This:
Combine all ingredients and shake. Pour your perfect BVI concoction into a tall glass, and don't forget to sprinkle freshly ground nutmeg on top. Garnish with an orange slice.

For a sample of what the perfect Painkiller should taste like, look no further than the Soggy Dollar Bar on Jost Van Dyke.

The Soggy Dollar, the creator of the Painkiller, mixes just the right combo of rum, pineapple and orange juice, along with a sprinkle of fresh nutmeg.

Y PAINKILLER THRILLER

The "Painkiller" has become so synonymous with BVI that it has transcended the bar scene, and can even be found in athletic pursuits. In fact, Pusser's "Painkiller Thriller" has emerged as the top windsurfing event in the British Virgin Islands. With four to six foot standing waves and winds reaching thirty knots, this windsurfing event takes competitors, traveling at twenty-five to thirty miles an hour, from Pusser's Marina Cay to Peg Leg Restaurant at Nanny Cay Marina. As the original rum of Great Britain's Royal Navy for 330 years, Pusser's Rum naturally provides each participant with a number of much needed Pusser's Painkillers to ease the pain of competition.

Y PUSSER'S PAINKILLER AT HOME

Pusser's Rum is known throughout BVI, and the Caribbean as a whole, partly due to the success of Pusser's Painkiller and Pusser's Grog. Though nothing beats the real thing, Pusser's has created a Painkiller Cocktail Mix, which uses all natural ingredients, so that vacationers can enjoy the rich flavor of their favorite cocktail once they've traveled home. Pusser's very appropriate tagline is, "Use the mix and save the pain!"

DISSECTING THE BUSHWHACKER

The tasty milkshake-like Bushwhacker recipe runs the gamut and may taste quite different depending on your seaside bar of choice. The one consistent element is that most Bushwhackers are based off of sweet liqueurs like Kahlua or Bailey's, mixed with a variety of light and dark liquors such as rum and vodka. For one of the best variations, try Potter's on Anegada. Ask for Mr. Potter to make the mighty concoction personally, a version that he calls "a whack in the bush."

THE DRINKING MAN'S GUIDE

If you're looking for an authentic guidebook for BVI drinkers, try The Drinking Man's Guide to BVI by Julian Putley. Brimming with drink recipes, limericks, and cartoons, this guide to all things tasty is a sure bet. For more tropical fun, try Malcolm Boyes' Tales of the Tropics, found at www.britishvirginbeer.com.

BUSHWHACKER

Ingredients:
1 oz Kahlua® coffee liqueur
1 oz Bailey's Irish Cream®
1 oz dark rum (or more)
4 oz cream of coconut (Coco Lopez)
4 oz half-and-half
2 cups ice
A small splash of vodka and a small splash of Grand Marnier (optional)

Locals Do It Like This:
Combine all ingredients into a blender and blend until the mixture takes on the consistency of a silky milkshake. Pour your tasty Bushwhacker into a tall glass and top with fresh ground nutmeg. Garnish with a cherry.

Note: For a more potent Bushwhacker, decrease the amount of cream of coconut and half and half. As you will soon discover, there are many ways to make this tasty concoction—explore them all. Try different variations and ingredients for best results.

LADY HAMILTON

Ingredients:
2 ounces Pusser's Rum
Equal parts orange juice
Equal parts passion fruit juice
Equal parts ginger ale
1 teaspoon fresh lime juice

Locals Do It Like This:
Mix together and enjoy over a tall glass of ice!

RUM PUNCH

Ingredients:
2 oz of white rum
1 oz lime guava
1 oz orange juice
1 oz pineapple juice
A touch of grenadine
Fresh nutmeg

Locals Do It Like This:
Mix together rum, guava, orange juice, and pineapple. Before serving add a splash of grenadine and sprinkle with nutmeg. Garnish with a slice of lime or orange.

 DARK AND STORMY

Ingredients:
2 ounces Goslings Black Seal rum
10 ounces of ginger beer
Lime wedge

Locals Do It Like This:
Sure the Dark and Stormy is the official drink of Bermuda, but island drinkers (especially boaters) have enjoyed this cocktail for decades no matter the island they call home. To make the perfect Dark and Stormy, fill a tall glass with ice and pour in the rum and then the ginger beer. Squeeze the lime wedge in the glass and lightly stir. Serve with another lime wedge as garnish.

Note: There's no beating Goslings Black Seal rum from Bermuda for this recipe.

LOCALS DO IT BEST

If you can find it, don't miss a sip of Callwood's Arundel rum, a secret recipe that is said to be all natural. Locals working at Callwood's Distillery in Cane Garden Bay claim that their rum does not produce headaches or hangovers because there are no preservatives or chemicals. Sold at eighty proof, the tasty raw rum is aged, mellowed, and only produced in small batches due to the fact that it is made from sugar cane juice (as opposed to molasses).

DARK AND STORMY REGATTA

From Trellis Bay, Beef Island to Anegada, the annual Dark and Stormy Regatta starts with a pre-race BBQ at De Loose Mongoose and finishes at Neptune's Treasure on Anegada. Participants report that the course between Anegada and Soper's Hole is always full of surprises! As an added bonus, pods of whales are often sighted along the way. Once ashore at Neptune's Treasure, participants are warmly greeted by the Soares family and other sponsors of the exciting race. A party ensues with drinks at the ready, horseshoe contests, dancing, and tons of local dishes shared.

NOT TO BE MISSED

℣ Drink Tip: Seek out a soursop for your next mixer! This local fruit is often blended with milk, vanilla essence, orange, pineapple, and rum.

♪ Local Celebrity Tip: If you're on Jost Van Dyke, seek out Foxy Callwood for sure. Foxy's Tamarind Bar, an open-air ramshackle of a hut, serves as a bar and social center. Not only does Foxy play a mean guitar and sing calypso ballads, but he's known for world-famous parties. In fact, the bar made Time magazine's list of "Top 5 Places to Spend New Year's."

♪ Music Video Tip: Want to pretend you're in a sunny music video? Then head on over to Ivan's on White Bay (Jost Van Dyke) where country star Kenny Chesney filmed "No Shoes, No Shirts, No Problems." Hangout with Ivan for the day and you'll see why ol' Kenny was inspired to write a song about his favorite hangout.

📄 Limin' Tip: There's no better source of local entertainment, tunes, events, and full moon info than Limin' Times. This free zine is picked up by more readers than any other weekly publication in the islands. Limin' can be snagged at points of entry, local markets, local restaurants, hotels, and many charter boat rentals. This puppy is brought to you by the fine folks at Island Publishing Services, the masterminds behind the Welcome Tourist Guide and Welcome Online. It's no wonder Limin' Times has been a source for local island info for 15 years. The Limin' Times also offers a popular web site, www.limin-times.com, which is updated every Thursday.

🛥 Overnight Anchorage Tip: The Willy T, a floating restaurant just off of Norman Island, serves as a popular overnight anchorage for the yachting community. Climb aboard this steel hundred-foot schooner for good eats, even better drinks, and unbeatable views from the aft bridge deck. Visit the William Thornton at www.williamthornton.com.

SIR FRANCIS DRAKE MARTINI

Ingredients:
3 parts pineapple juice
2 parts Vanilla Vodka
1 part Grand Marnier
Fresh orange juice
Twist of orange peel

Locals Do It Like This:
As always, start by chilling your favorite martini glass by filling it with ice and letting it stand for five minutes. Meanwhile, fill a martini shaker half full with ice. Add vodka, pineapple juice, and Grand Marnier. Shake thoroughly to chill. Remove and discard the ice from your martini glass and strain your tropical martini from the shaker. Top with just a splash of orange juice and an orange peel. Serve immediately, as cold as possible.

 REEF JUICE

Ingredients:
1½ oz rum
1 oz banana liqueur
½ oz gin
½ oz lime juice (unsweetened)
2 oz pineapple juice
Splash of grenadine

Locals Do It Like This:
Combine all ingredients, mix, and pour in tall glass. Garnish with a pineapple and lime.

BEWARE OF THE ZEUS JUICE

Looking for a bartender that can mix it all? Then try Zeus! As a master BVI mixologist, Zeus routinely serves up tropical concoctions at Willy T in the Norman Island Bight. Zeus, who has been the feature of several consumer publications, hangs his publicity shots behind the bar where he makes his famous "Zeus Juice." Toss a compliment or two his way, and Zeus is likely to stiffen his famous BVI cocktail.

LISTEN TO QUITO:

Growing up on Tortola, Quito Rymer has always been in tune with his island and its rich culture. A BVI hometown hero, this legend in the making first sharpened his artistic talents through painting and drawing. His career began in the church halls of Cane Garden Bay. Teaching himself to play the guitar, Quito began to compose both lyrics and music. Today Quito plays both as a solo act and with his band, "The Edge." Throughout his musical rise to fame, Quito has opened for Third World, Freddie McGregor, and Ziggy Marley. BVIslanders and tourists alike enjoy Quito's tunes on Tuesdays and Thursdays and can hear him play solo as guests enjoy their dinner and drinks overlooking Cane Garden Bay. On Fridays and Saturdays you can also hear Quito Rymer and The Edge play for a crowd ready for dancing and singing at Quito's Gazebo.

To date Quito has released:
Quito Rymer - Reggae Express
Quito Rymer - Mix Up World
Quito Rymer - Searching
Quito Rymer & The Edge - Paradise
Quito Rymer - Caribbean Run
Quito Rymer & The Edge - Iron Strong
Quito Rymer - Quito Unplugged
For more, visit: www.quitorymer.com

Can't Find A Bar? Many beach bars can be contacted by ship-to-shore radio on VHF 16.

If You Don't Drink Anything Else, Drink the Rum: Clearly the Caribbean is the epicenter of world rum production—so drink up while in the BVI's, you'll find local varieties of light rum made from column stills.

Try The Big Banana:
One of the coziest bars in all the islands, the Big Banana (also known as Paradise Club, 284-495-4606) is home to the famous concoction of the same name—the Big Banana house drink made of fine rum, Bailey's, coconut cream, and, of course, a banana.

Best Place For Mango Bellini:
Capriccio di Mare, Road Town, Tortola (284-494-5369). Brought to you by the owners of Brandywine Bay Restaurant, this local favorite is home to the best mango bellini, a variation of the famous champagne-based cocktail served at Harry's Bar in Venice.

Nominate Your Favorite Bar Buddy:
Visit www.islandlowdown.com to nominate your favorite seaside watering hole, bartender, or drinking buddy.

If you don't drink anything else in BVI, drink the rum.

NAVY GROG

Ingredients:
2 oz rum
¼ oz falernum liqueur
1 oz orange juice
1 oz pineapple juice
1 oz guava nectar
½ oz fresh lime juice

Locals Do It Like This:
Mix all ingredients and pour over a cup of ice. No garnish required. A plastic cup is perfectly acceptable!

CANNONBALL

Ingredients:
2 oz rum
Angostura Bitters

Locals Do It Like This:
This one is quite simple: pour the rum over a cup of ice, and add a few dashes of bitters.

▮ FEELING GROGGY?

Known as "Old Grogram," British Admiral Vernon was famous for ordering his daily ration of rum, diluted with water, during his tenure in the mid 1700s. His men quickly came to call the mixture "grog," and pegged any sailor who drank too much grog as "groggy."

▮ RUM SHENANIGANS

Admiral Vernon's infamous Order to Captains no. 349 on August 21, 1740:

"… unanimous opinion of both Captains and Surgeons that the pernicious custom of the seaman drinking their allowance of rum in drams, and often at once, is attended with many fatal effects to their morals as well as their health … besides the ill consequences of stupifying [sic] their rational qualities … You are hereby required and directed … that the respective daily allowance … be every day mixed with the proportion of a quart of water to a half pint of rum, to be mixed in a scuttled butt kept for that purpose, and to be done upon the deck, and in the presence of the Lieutenant of the Watch who is to take particular care to see that the men are not defrauded in having their full allowance of rum … and let those that are good husbanders receive extra lime juice and sugar that it be made more palatable to them."

The Best Swim-Up Bar

The Dog and Dolphin Bar & Grill on Virgin Gorda (284-494-8000, Web site: www.nailbay.com/dining. htm). This peaceful poolside eatery offers sunset views and a swim-up bar with a mean rum punch. Afterwards, take a dip in the Jacuzzi and consider never going home.

The Best Bar for Honest Drinkers

Ivan's Honest Bar on Jost Van Dyke (284-495-9358). Ivan's features an "honor bar," giving patrons a chance to play bartender. Located on White Bay, you'll want to check out Ivan's digs on a Thursday or Friday night when live music is at its peak. Be sure to sign your tab and pay before leaving; Ivan trusts you!

The Best Bar for Pilots

Flying Iguana on Virgin Gorda (284-495-5277). An open-air drinking destination that overlooks the Atlantic Ocean, the Iguana sits next to the airport, making it a favorite for pilots and passengers arriving or departing Virgin Gorda.

The Best BVI Bartender

Here we have a tie between Edith, the bartender at Mad Dog on Virgin Gorda (284-495-5830), and Lincoln, the bartender/owner at The Mine Shaft on Virgin Gorda (284-495-5260). World famous for her secret pina colada recipe, Edith's drinks are simply unbeatable. Though she may be quite quiet at first, Edith has one of the best smiles on the island and can fill your day with barside stories about the BVI's. Likewise, Lincoln at The Mine Shaft has never met a stranger. He'll charm you with his welcoming style while mixing up a mean house favorite, called the "Cave In." Ask him if you can wear one of the helmets hanging above the bar and tip up his famous spiked cocktail.

The Best Bar for Sailors

Just dingy up to the one-hundred foot dock and join the fun. Jolly Roger's outside bar offers live entertainment, good eats, and even allows boaters to send a fax or simply stock up on ice. (284-495-4559)

Just look for the Jolly Roger flag, and you'll be treated to good drinks and tasty eats.

FOG CUTTER

Ingredients:
2 oz rum
½ oz gin
½ oz brandy
1 oz orange juice
3 tbsp lemon juice
1 tbsp orgeat (syrup made from almonds, sugar and rose water/orange-flower water)
Splash of sherry

Locals Do It Like This:
Mix ingredients and pour over a glass of ice. It was, however, originally made with a barley and almond blend. Add a splash of sherry on top.

 KEY LIME MARTINI

Ingredients:
4 oz key lime vodka (try Charbay)
2 oz vodka
2 tbsp fresh lime juice
1 tbsp cool whip
2 thick slices of lime
2 martini glasses, rimmed with sugar (try lime cocktail candy sugar)

Locals Do It Like This:
Chill two martini glasses. Next, fill a martini shaker half full with ice. Add your favorite vodka and then cool whip, and shake. Retrieve your chilled glasses and line the rim with lime candy sugar (optional). Strain your mighty concoction into the two chilled martini glasses, and top with lime juice. Add a touch of cool whip (optional).

WHAT IS ORGEAT SYRUP?

Made from almonds, sugar, and rose/orange flower water, orgeat syrup is a sweet blend that is used to flavor many cocktails. Originally made with a barley and almond blend, orgeat syrup is hard to find, but worth the search.

WHAT IS KEY LIME ANYWAY?

Key lime (citrus aurantifolia), also known as the West Indian lime, is considered by many as "true lime." The Key lime tree, which is limited to warm subtropical climates, produces a lime that is much smaller than most limes. Extremely tart, the Key lime is highly flavorful. Introduced to the Caribbean by the Spaniards, its unique flavor has resulted in everything from Key lime pie to Key lime martinis.

The Best Garden Setting

Lobster Trap on Anegada (284-495-8466). Positioned on the main anchorage's beachfront, this garden eatery is home to what else but local Anegada lobster served barbeque style. The setting is quaint, quiet, and not to be missed.

The Best Place to Drink with Ex-Pats

Rock Café on Virgin Gorda (284-495-5482). Perched on a rock at the traffic circle in The Valley on Virgin Gorda, Rock Café is a popular gathering spot for travelers who never quite made it home. Living the dream, these regulars often opt for the air-conditioned bar on the first floor of the café, while tourists often dine among the breathtaking boulders on the top floor.

The Best Place for a Burger During Overnight Moorings

Sand Box on Prickly Pear Island (284-495-9122). This is a casual beachside watering hole with a great selection of burgers, beer, and cocktails.

The Best Place for Late Night Cravings

Stanley's on Tortola (284-495-9424). Located in Cane Garden Bay, Stanley's is always open late, with a full menu of fresh fish, steaks, burgers, and lobster.

Best Place to Watch the Sunset

Head over to the Cooper Island Beach Club (800-542-4624), a popular restaurant on beautiful Manchioneel Beach.

Best Do-It-Yourself Bar

Harris Place (284-495-9302), located in Little Harbor, boasts not only the largest lobsters in town but also the best "do-it-yourself" bar. Built by the late Harris Jones, Harris Place is run by the Jones family and is home to all-you-can-eat buffets, a secret family hot sauce, and excellent pea soup. The real show stopper, however, is the laid-back bar which allows patrons to make their own drinks any way that strikes their fancy.

The Best "In" Place to See and Be Seen

Foxy's Taboo (284-495-0218) is located on Diamond Cay, just a short drive from the original Foxy's in Great Harbour. Run by BVI superstar Foxy Callwood's daughter, Foxy's Taboo has emerged into the happening spot to see and be seen. Good food, the drinks flow readily (excellent wine selection), and plenty of celebrity sightings. Moorings available.

The Best Singing Chef

The Last Resort (284-495-2520), located on an islet in Trellis Bay, Beef Island. This hot spot dishes not only a solid dinner menu full of local seafood but also a comedy/music show with diners joining in the fun (and receiving free shots). Though longtime entertainment legend Tony Snell is no longer wowing the crowds, his daughter and son-in-law are holding up their end of the bargain. Excellent live entertainment is found here each night.

BVI LULLABY

Ingredients:
1 oz rum
1 oz coconut rum
1 oz pineapple juice
1 oz guava nectar
½ oz sugar syrup
½ oz lemon juice

Locals Do It Like This:
Mix ingredients and pour over crushed ice. Garnish with lime, pineapple, and orange.

MANGO-TINI

Ingredients:
4 oz mango rum
4 oz vanilla rum
1 tsp of cointreau
2 oz fresh orange juice
1 Madagascar vanilla bean (opt for a Mexican vanilla bean if you can find it)
2 tbsp of heavy cream
2 frozen mango spears
2 chilled martini glasses

Locals Do It Like This:
Chill large martini glasses. Fill a shaker half full with ice. Divide the vanilla bean in half and scrape the insides of the bean into the shaker. Add the rum, cointreau, and orange juice into the mix, and shake. Next add the heavy cream into the shaker and lightly swirl the concoction. Strain the contents into the martini glasses, adding a frozen mango spear for garnish.

♥ A ROMANTIC VIEW

Head to Carrot Bay where you'll find Bananakeet Cafe at the Heritage Inn. Sipping your favorite island delight, this eatery's view is unbeatable. Perched high on the bluff next to Carrot Bay, Bananakeet (284-4945842) overlooks the water toward Long Bay and Jost Van Dyke. A popular happy hour is complete with local tunes and a gourmet menu.

♫ LOCAL MUSICIANS/BANDS

Carl Williams: Often plays at Rock Café.
Dennis Stevens: Look for him at Little Dix or Biras Creek.
Desmond Daily: Try Marina Cay.
Faze 2: Chez Bamboo, Little Dix Bay, Bath and Turtle.
Hiyah Version: Bomba Shack's Full Moon Parties, as well as Myett's.
Hudson and the Hoo Doo Cats: Try them at Jolly Roger.
Leon and the Hotshots: Finding them at Little Dix Bay is a good bet.
Michael Beans: Look for him at Marina Cay.
MJ Blues: Find them at the Pub or Myett's.
Philip Thomas: Check out De Loose Mongoose or Jolly Roger.
Quito (Solo): Where else, Quito's Gazebo.
Quito and the Edge: Of course, Quito's Gazebo.
Ras Rio: Find them at Big Banana.
Marvin Sprauve & Focus Band: Born on Virgin Gorda, Marvin is a popular veteran musician that is often enjoyed at Bomba Shack and Jolly Roger.

BEST PERSON TO HAVE A BEER WITH IN THE BVI:

Award-winning journalist, Malcolm Boyes, a BVI fixture, is known as an island drink-master. In a former life, Malcolm, affectionately known as "Manpot" in the islands, was a producer of the television show Extra, a journalist for Britain's prestigious Fleet Street News Agency, a reporter for the BBC's "Radio London," and a special correspondent for Time Inc's People magazine.

Found most often with a Red Stripe in hand at Tortola's favorite party destination, Bomba Shack, Malcolm can spin one hell of a tale, laced with real-life adventures working for Paramount TV's Hard Copy, REAL TV, and Entertainment Tonight.

Following his lifetime dream of creative writing, Malcolm is now authoring a series of outrageous and enjoyable stories of the Caribbean in his book, Tales of the Tropics.

Malcolm Boyes can be most easily tracked down on "Travel Talk Online" (www.traveltalkonline.com) in the BVI section of the Web site. Invite him to share a brew with you and you're in for a real treat.

BEST PEOPLE TO CHAT WITH ONLINE IN BVI:

Walker and Nancy Mangum, operators of www.bvipirate.com and www.nwmangum.com, are Texas transplants now living life as BVI beach bums. Their keen insight into the islands, observations, photographs, recipes, and tips are all chronicled online for the world to enjoy. The Mangums call Cow Wreck Beach home and often write about their love for BVI on their sites, as well as on www.traveltalkonline.com. Walker Mangum reportedly discovered BVI while bare boating in 1987 when he spent one night anchored at Anegada. He now is a seasoned traveler to BVI, and he shows off his prowess with gifts to new vacationers–such tidbits as recipes for his "Turbo Painkiller," travel advice, and fly fishing tips.

BEST BVI PAINTER

Roger Ellis' dazzling Caribbean colors and brilliant light are just a few of the reasons to seek out this BVI legend. Renowned for his accuracy and beautiful BVI maps, he captures BVI life like no other, while his affinity for the islands as a whole is played out in his marine conservation efforts. For many years the islands have been his home, with commissions coming in from around the world as he paints in his studio and gallery by the edge of the sea. To view Roger's creations, contact Flukes Design at 284-495-2043.

BEST FOLKS TO SHARE A CUP OF JOE WITH ON THE ISLANDS

Phillip and Anne Fenty, owners of D'Best Cup coffee shop, offer some the finest java available in the British Virgin Islands. You can buy fresh ground coffee beans or just sit around and enjoy good conversation with the owners and other regulars who frequent their outdoor patio. You might also want to try a tostada or a good ol' fashioned hot dog with a yummy milk shake! They have teas, pastries, smoothies, and milkshakes. Also serving breakfast and lunch. Open from 6:30 am. (284-495-0259)

BEST PERSON TO TAKE CARE OF FIDO IN BVI

Tessa Gunter, a founding member of the Humane Society in the British Virgin Islands, has provided shelter and care for injured animals and strays for over three decades. Tessa is dedicated to getting animals off the streets and then integrating animals back into the community through responsible adoption. The Humane Society receives no government assistance and instead is supported purely by the hard work of Tessa and her assistant, Vijay Bissoondutt. They also run a boarding and grooming facility to cover the cost of overhead. Look for Tessa at the many fundraising events, yard sales, gaming nights, and dog shows that she organizes throughout the islands. Tessa Gunter and the Humane Society can be reached at 284-494-2284 or www.bvihumanesociety.org.

RUM RUNNER—BVI STYLE

Ingredients:
1 oz dark rum
1 oz light rum
½ oz blackberry liqueur
¼ oz banana liqueur
Splash of grenadine syrup
Splash of lime juice
1½ cups of ice

Locals Do It Like This:
Mix the rum and liqueur in a blender with ice. Pour into a tall glass and garnish with an orange slice or cherry.

COCONUT MARTINI

Ingredients:
6 oz chilled vodka
1 Madagascar vanilla bean
1 tbsp cream of coconut
1 tsp coconut flakes

Locals Do It Like This:
Chill two large martini glasses with just a dash of cream of coconut at the bottom. Fill a shaker half full with ice. Divide the vanilla bean in half and scrape the insides into the shaker. Add the vodka and the remaining cream of coconut. Shake, and shake some more! Strain the shaker's contents into the martini glasses. Garnish with coconut flakes (fresh flakes if possible).

Y DE GOOSE IS LOOSE

On tiny Beef Island, De Losse Mongoose (284-495-2303) is a water-side sipping hole that sits next to the main island and is connected to Tortola. As part of the Beef Island Guest House on Trellis Bay, you'll find a variety of island cocktails along with an excellent happy hour and a popular Sunday night barbeque.

◇ CUBAN CIGARS

For Cuban cigars in the islands you'll want to head over to Little Denmark (284-494-2455) on Tortola. Duck into the room-size humidor and sample their extensive collection of Cohiba, Montocristo, Hoyo de Monterrey, Partagas, H. Upmann, and Romeo Y Julieta. While at Little Denmark, make sure to chat with its owner, Diana Bruce, a BVIslander with a long history in the business. In fact, Diana's father opened a cigarette factory on picturesque Peter Island in the 1930s. Cuban cigars can also be purchased at such places as Bobby's, Riteway, and One Mart in Road Town. On Virgin Gorda you'll want to try the Tropical Gift Collections or the Caribbean Flavor Gift Shop. Many resorts, such as Katitche Point, also provide Cuban cigars for guests. As with any Cuban cigar purchase, there are many ways to tell if a box and the cigars are authentic—from the date codes and the bands to the smell of the tobacco and the color of the wrapper.

KING OF THE CARIBBEAN

Carib Lager—In the Caribbean, this beer is considered the golden nectar of the Gods. When you taste this brew, you taste a lifestyle of white sands, clear seas, calypso, and trade winds. Its light taste and medium fill makes Carib the only choice while in the British Virgin Islands.

Kick It Up A Notch:

Carib, the legendary beer of the Caribbean, is unbeatable. However, if you really want to add a punch to this hometown brew, BVI experts will tell you to snag a bottle of Bacardi Limon rum in lieu of the age-old beer-lime combo. Add a tug of "Limon" to your brew, place a thumb over the rim, and invert slowly.

Or Make it into a Sauce:

Island kitchen whizzes know that the always refreshing Carib can morph into a tangy island barbeque sauce when just the right touch is applied. To make your own Carib Barbeque Sauce, mix ¾ cub Carib beer with 8 ounces of canned tomato sauce, 1 cup chopped onions, ½ brown sugar, 3 tbsps Worcestershire sauce, 2 tsps salt, and ¼ tsp of fresh black pepper. Mmmm, beer and island barbeque—it just doesn't get any better than this.

The golden nectar of the Gods.

BEST BEACH BARS:

- Anegada Reef Hotel on Anegada (284-495-8002). Reservations required by 4 PM. Web site: www. anegadareef.com

- Bomba's Shack on Tortola at Apple and Cappoons Bay. A beachside shack known worldwide for its Full Moon Parties, "Mushroom Tea," live entertainment, and outrageous fun.

- Rob White on Pusser's Marina Cay. A small islet that offers live music, Pusser's Company Store and Restaurant, and, of course, lots of rum! Web site: http://www.pussers.com/outposts/marinacay

- Rudy's Bar on Jost Van Dyke at Great Harbour (284-495-9282). This hidden gem is found in the west end of Great Harbour. The perfect island watering hole, Rudy's boasts free flowing drinks and some of the best lobster in the BVI's.

- Soggy Dollar Bar on Jost Van Dyke at White Bay (284-495-9888). Home to the "Painkiller," Soggy Dollar Bar is one of the most talked about BVI destinations, serving the best drinks in all of the islands. Dinner or lunch on the beachfront ain't bad either!

- Bath & Turtle on Virgin Gorda at The Valley (284-495-5239). Head to this hopping patio destination in Yacht Harbour for its weekly "Jump Up," and you'll see why this Caribbean eatery is known just as much for its seafood as it is for its local tunes.

Courtesy of William Thornton Restaurant and Bar

Thirsty patrons enjoy a Willy T education.

♫ LIVE MUSIC

Keep an eye peeled, if you see any one of these local bands playing in BVI—make sure to attend:

Impulse—unbeatable reggae, a must-see.
Focus—everything from soft rock to calypso.
Latitude Stars—classic calypso/reggae with a romantic flair.
Romeo and the Injectors—steel band.
Lonely Man One Man—solid calypso, reggae, and rock.
Morris Mark—a solo act with a strong calypso influence.
Natural Mystic—BVI jazz.
Lover Boys—straight up fungi.
O-2—top 40.
Paradise Roots—the best soca.
Lashing Dogs—a popular fungi band in the BVI, with a number of CDs to boot.
Reflections—steel band.

HUNTER B'S LIME & COCONUT:

Ingredients:
14 oz cream of coconut
7 oz coconut milk
½ cup lime juice
7 oz coconut rum

Locals Do It Like This:
Blend this tasty concoction and top with a cherry and freshly grated coconut.

This recipe is courtesy of Hunter Butler, Blue Escapes Villa Rentals, www.blueescapes.com.

MANGO MARGARITA

Ingredients:
1 ¼ cups mango, cubed
6 oz tequila
6 oz sour mix
2 oz Triple Sec
Ice

Locals Do It Like This:
Combine the tequila, sour mix, and Triple Sec, then cut the mango and blend for 10-15 seconds. Top with ice and blend to the desired consistency.

FAVORITE FINDS

Cow Wreck Beach Bar on Anegada (284-495-9461). You can't beat the Cow Wreck—the best spot for fresh lobster on the beach and a cold beer. Try the conch, shell fish, and ribs too!

Chez Bamboo on Virgin Gorda (284-495-5752). Creole meets Caribbean. Try the poulet au citron, and don't miss the tasty deserts.

Clem's By the Sea on Tortola (284-495-4350). In the North Shore across from Carrot Bay. Your best bet is the rice and peas on a Monday night when you can enjoy a local steel band and a wide selection of island concoctions.

Quito's Gazebo on Tortola (284-495-4837). Head down on a Wednesday night for Quito's incredible fish fry and live local music. Quito is a bar-side fixture, cranking out original tunes and a number of mixed beverages and West Indian plates.

Sebastian's On the Beach on Tortola (284-495-4212). Located in Cappoons Bay, this beachfront hangout is popular among lobster-chomping tourists and locals seeking Sebastian's West Indian specialties. The smart money is on Thursday night when some of the freshest lobster is offered. Go early, the house packs fast.

Rhymers on Tortola (284-495-4639). Located in Cane Garden Bay, Rhymers has a fine lobster special on Thursdays, and one heck of a breakfast served daily.

Sand Box Seafood Grille & Bar on Prickly Pear Island, North Sound, near Virgin Gorda (284-495-9123 or call on VHF Channel 16). Check out this eatery for a killer grilled Mahi-mahi sandwich, or try their signature "Shrimp Prickly Pear."

Rudy's Mariner's on Jost Van Dyke (284-495-9282) is home to some of the best local fish around.

Thelma's Hide Out on Virgin Gorda (284-495-5646). Thelma King dishes up authentic island creations at this tiny roadside gem. A popular spot for locals to play darts and listen to live music, Thelma's Hide Out offers casual outdoor seating and home-style goodies such as West Indian stews, mutton, and fish.

Wendell's World on Jost Van Dyke (284-495-9259) offers simple snacks on the beach at Great Harbour, along with a killer honey-dipped-chicken recipe.

The Dove Restaurant & Wine Bar on Tortola (284-494-0313) offers one heck of a wine list served in a historic West Indian cottage.

Giorgio's Table on Virgin Gorda (284-495-5684) provides an intimate setting along with tasty pasta dishes, veal, and beef filet.

Lazy Iguana on Peter Island (284-494-2449) serves local BVI specialties on a hidden beach in Buttonwood Bay.

Rita's Bar & Restaurant on Tortola (284-494-6165) dishes an unbeatable homemade West Indian soup.

Nominate Your Own Favorite Find: www.islandlowdown.com

Saba Rock Resort on Saba Rock (284-495-7711, Web site www.sabarock.com). Located on a tiny island known as Saba Rock, this bar and café offers straight-up pub grub in an eye-popping setting.

Crab Hole on Virgin Gorda (284-495-5307). You have to try the callaloo at this home-style café in the South Valley.

Fischer's Cove Beach Hotel on Virgin Gorda (284-495-5252). Fischer's Cove offers one of the best sunset views in all of the BVI's. Sit back, order a cocktail, and relax at this quiet beachside dining destination. The chef serves a mean curry lobster too!

Leverick Bay Restaurant on Virgin Gorda (Web site: www.therestaurantatleverickbay.com). Head for the upstairs terrace for a cocktail and an amazing view. Offering excellent happy hour deals, if there is still room you may want to stick around for their popular rack of lamb.

Top of the Baths on Virgin Gorda (284-495-5497). A spectacular view, Top of the Baths sits at no other than the very tip-top of what else but The Baths. Though the restaurant is popular with tourists hoping to get their first glance at the natural rock formations nearby, this open air eatery is also one of the best spots for a Bushwhacker, local conch fritters, and an unbeatable view.

Pirate's Bight on Norman Island (284-496-7827 or on VHF Channels 16 and 69). Check out the only restaurant (on land) in the Bight of Norman Island for an unbeatable buffet of local offerings. Local calypso bands, dancing, and all-you-can-eat island fare.

Donovan's Reef on Scrub Island (284-495-2508 or VHF Channel 16). Dinghy over (it's the only way) to this hidden gem that is brimming with lobster and local goodies.

The Indians

LOOKING FOR SOMETHING A BIT MORE FANCY

Biras Creek on Virgin Gorda (284-494-355, Web site: www.biras.com). This upscale destination overlooks the North Sound and offers some of the most elegant cuisine and cocktails in all of the BVI's. Though its four-course prix fixe menu is not to be missed, simply ordering a cocktail and taking in the sights is worth the trip alone.

Bitter End Yacht Club on Virgin Gorda (284-494-2746). This popular clubhouse for yachtsmen, known as yachties, sits proudly on the Gorda Sound. Serving up a mean lobster with all the West Indian sides you can imagine, these upscale digs should always make your list.

Little Dix Bay Resort on Virgin Gorda (284-495-05555, Web site: www.littledixbay.com). Considered the original luxury resort in all of the BVI's, Little Dix offers a breathtaking dining terrace under a pavilion-style roof. Lunch is à la carte, with dinner a bit more dressy.

Devil's Bay, Virgin Gorda

Chapter 5

Sweet Tooth

🍾 COCONUT RUM
SUGGESTIONS

A touch of coconut rum makes everybody's favorite BVI Banana Pudding kick! Try a dab of one of the following:

🍾 Captain Morgan's Parrot Bay
🍾 Cabana Boy Pineapple Coconut Rum
🍾 CocoRibe
🍾 Coco Mania Coconut Jamaica Rum
🍾 Tortuga Coconut Rum
🍾 Cruzan Coconut Rum
🍾 Malibu Coconut Rum
🍾 Whaler's Coconut Rum
🍾 Maui Dark Coconut Rum

🌍 KEEP IT LOCAL

To keep it local—from your produce to your booze—seek out the Callwood Distillery in Cane Garden Bay. This potstill, made of stone and brick, dates back to the mid-1700s. Operated by the Callwood family since the late 1800s, this is true artisan rum. The family-made rum is concocted with sugar cane and no preservatives, then processed in small batches through a press mill where the sugar juice is squeezed into copper pots and boiled. Once boiled down, water is added and it's fermented in oak barrels. Finally, the fermented liquid is boiled again and cooled in copper tubing and then stored for up to four years.

 BVI BANANA PUDDING

Ingredients:
12 bananas, mashed
2 tbsp butter
¼ cup brown sugar
½ cup flour
¼ cup coconut milk, or cream
½ tsp nutmeg
¼ cup coconut rum

Locals Do It Like This:
To make this classic recipe you'll want to start by mashing the bananas. Next, mix together the butter and the sugar before adding the bananas and flour. Stir in the nutmeg, and then add the coconut milk and coconut rum. Stir. Pour contents into a large pan (9 x 11 pan works best) and bake at 350° for one hour. Top with fresh cream.

 BANANA FLAMBÉ

Ingredients:
2 bananas
4 tablespoons sugar
½ cup white rum
1 lime

Locals Do It Like This:
Halve the bananas lengthwise, and brown them over medium heat in oil in a frying pan for approximately five minutes on each side. Next, add the rum and the sugar, while cooking for an additional five minutes on each side. Add a dash of lime juice and serve immediately.

CARIBBEAN COCONUT ICE CREAM

Ingredients:
2 cups heavy cream
1 cup milk
2 cups coconut water
1 cup coconut meat, jelly
2 egg yolks
1 cup sugar

Locals Do It Like This:
Start by bringing the coconut water to a boil. Let approximately one cup evaporate and set aside. Combine the cream and milk to the reduced coconut water. Bring to a slight boil again over medium heat for 5 to 7 minutes. Meanwhile, beat the egg yolks and sugar together. Gradually add the hot cream mixture to the beaten yolks and sugar mixture. Continue to stir at all times so that the liquid does not curdle. Cook the mixture on low heat until thick, then remove from heat and cool completely. Once the custard has cooled you may add the ground coconut jelly. Place in the freezer for approximately two hours (an ice-cream maker will work too) and then remove in order to break up any ice crystals that have formed. Place the custard back in the freezer for another two hours. You may need to break up ice crystals again to keep it silky smooth.

COCONUT WATER

A natural isotonic beverage, coconut water offers the same level of electrolytic balance as we have in our blood. This "fluid of life" is often siphoned directly and is widely known to be more nutritious than milk and orange juice. Naturally sterile, coconut milk permeates through the filtering husk and offers far more potassium than most sports drinks, and much less sodium!

COCONUT TIDBITS

◇ The fleshy part of the coconut seed is edible and is used fresh, as well as dried, in many recipes.
◇ Mature coconuts have less liquid than young coconuts.
◇ Coconut milk is made by processing grated coconut with hot water (or milk).
◇ When refrigerated, coconut cream will rise to the top and separate from the milk.
◇ Leftover fibre from coconut milk can be used to feed livestock.
◇ Coconut water can be used as intravenous fluid.
◇ Coconut can be used for making potting compost.
◇ Leaves can be used for roofing thatch.
◇ Coconut husks and shells can be used for fuel as well as charcoal.

WHY SO MUCH NUTMEG IN BVI?

The fragrant nutmeg was brought from Indonesia to Grenada, the "isle of spice," by an English sea captain. The evergreen produces nutmeg, the actual seed of a tree that today is sold in local BVI markets. In the islands, nutmeg can be used in everything from jerk seasoning (Scotch bonnet, onions, scallions, Jamaican pimento, thyme, and cinnamon) to desserts (ice cream) and the perfect topping for tropical cocktails (Bushwhacker and Painkiller).

TRY THESE SWEET TREATS

- Try the BVI Rum Fried Bananas at Jolly Roger Inn (284-495-4559) on Tortola.
- Try the chocolate bourbon mint cake at Chez Bamboo (284-495-5752) on Virgin Gorda.
- Try the crème brûlée at La Cabanon (284-494-8600) on Tortola.
- Try the tiramisu at Giorgio's Table (800-832-2302) on Virgin Gorda.
- Try any of the homemade desserts from scratch at Marlene's (284-494-4634) on Tortola.
- Try the "Famoose Brownie" at De Loose Mongoose (284-495-2303) on Beef Island.
- Try the Raspberry Mango Cheese Cake at the Top of the Baths (284-495-5497) on Virgin Gorda.

 FRESH NUTMEG ICE CREAM

Ingredients:
1 ½ cups milk
1 ½ cups heavy cream
3 eggs
¾ cup sugar
1 tsp fresh nutmeg, grated
¼ tsp vanilla

Locals Do It Like This:
Bring one cup of milk and cream to a boil in a saucepan, while whisking the nutmeg, eggs, sugar, and vanilla with ½ cup of milk together in a separate bowl. Next, add the milk mixture into the egg mixture to form a custard. Cook the custard over medium heat until the mixture is thick, making sure to stir in order to prevent curdling. Remove from heat and cool the custard. Place in the freezer for approximately two hours (an ice-cream maker will work too) and then remove in order to break up any ice crystals that have formed. Place the custard back in the freezer for another two hours. You may need to break up ice crystals again to keep it silky smooth.

 FLAMING MANGOES

Ingredients:
2 fresh mangoes
1 cup freshly squeezed orange juice
2 tablespoons sugar
1 cup 151 Rum

Locals Do It Like This:
Begin by cutting the fresh mangoes into slices and placing them in a skillet. Pour the freshly squeezed orange juice over the fruit and sprinkle with sugar. Allow to simmer, and then begin gently stirring to coat the fruit for approximately four minutes. Pour in the 151 Rum while keeping the mangoes over medium heat. Next is the fun part, flame your tasty sauce by pouring the rum into a teaspoon and holding it over a flame until it ignites. Use the flaming rum to then light the rum poured on top of the mangoes. This superb dessert is best served over homemade vanilla ice cream!

 BVI BAKED BANANAS

Ingredients:
4 ripe bananas
2 tbsp cinnamon powder
1 tbsp fresh nutmeg
2 tbsp vanilla extract
1 cup sugar
4 cups water

Locals Do It Like This:
Peel the bananas and place them in boiling water. Add the vanilla extract, nutmeg, sugar, cinnamon, and water and boil for 15 to 20 minutes. Next, remove the banana mixture and bake in the oven for approximately 10 more minutes. BVI baked bananas are simply awesome when combined with homemade ice-cream!

 GUAVA ICE CREAM

Ingredients:
12 ripe guavas
2 cans evaporated milk
1 can condensed milk
2 tablespoons of cornstarch

Locals Do It Like This:
Cut the guavas and boil for forty-five minutes. Next, strain the guava juice and thicken it with the corn starch. Then add milk and sweeten this tasty concoction to your liking. Freeze your fine guava creation until ready to serve.

SCORE SOME ICE CREAM HERE:

- The Rock Café (284-495-5482) on Virgin Gorda dishes Poire Belle Helene (cooked pears served with vanilla ice cream and chocolate sauce), Ice Cream Caia (vanilla ice cream topped with chocolate sauce, whipped cream, and a cherry), and Baileys Affogato (vanilla ice cream drowned with Baileys liqueur).
- Tradewinds Restaurant (800-346-4451) on Peter Island is the home of the famed Caribbean Snowball, homemade vanilla ice cream swimming in chocolate sauce and covered in white chocolate and coconut coating.
- Midtown Restaurant (284-494-2764) on Tortola, run by the ever so popular Gloria, offers coconut ice cream as the perfect ending to a hefty helping of local dishes.
- Al Martin Ice Cream on Soper's Hole offers a solid selection of flavors and other sweet treats.
- Jewel's Snack Shop (284-495-9286) on Jost Van Dyke scoops up an unbeatable mango sherbet.
- La Dolce Vita (284-494-8770) on Tortola, near the roundabout in Road Town, provides homemade Italian ice cream.
- Big Bamboo (284-499-1680), on Anegada is known for its freshly caught lobster and conch, but make sure to save room for some of its tasty ice cream before hitting the beach.
- Biras Creek (877-883-0756), on Virgin Gorda is home to Chef Vikram Garg, the mastermind behind a killer Chocolate mousse Savarin with curry caramel and caramel ice cream. Try this one with a glass of Herzstuck Riesling Spatlese from Weingut Kirsten.

¥ AFTER DINNER DRINKS

Sydney's Peace and Love: Check out the well-stocked, self-serve bar to create your own cordial dessert drink. Just remember that your after-dinner concoction is on the honor system here.

Guana Island: After feasting on island delicacies by Linus and Dwight at the private resort on Guana Island, the discrete staff politely serves after-dinner cordials in the living room.

Foxy's Bar: If you're looking for a more casual way to spend the evening, head over to Foxy's for an after dinner cocktail that can be enjoyed as you dance in the sand as Foxy plays island tunes on his guitar.

¥ COCKTAILS ON A PRIVATE CHARTER

Whether it's a crewed yacht or a bareboat charter, BVI has you covered. Just take your pick: catamaran, monohull, or super luxury yacht. No matter your charter service of choice, there's nothing better than enjoying an after-dinner cocktail on board just before you tie up to a mooring for the night. To get the lowdown on the BVI charter industry, check out the Marine Association of the British Virgin Islands at www.marinebvi.com or 284-494-2751.

¥ NO HANGOVER COCKTAILS

Many residents and tourists will boast that the fine rum made at the local Callwood Distillery does not cause hangovers (or your money back). And in fact, there might just be something to this local legend, as Callwood's Arundel All Natural Rum is made in super small batches and has no chemicals or preservatives. As if drinking rum couldn't get any better, Callwood's even uses recycled liquor bottles.

TROPICAL FRUIT DRIZZLED WITH CHOCOLATE SAUCE

Ingredients:
4 cups assorted fresh tropical fruit
3 tablespoons orange-flavored liqueur
6 ounces semisweet chocolate chips
½ cup granulated sugar
½ cup evaporated milk
2 teaspoons butter
1 tablespoon orange-flavored rum

Locals Do It Like This:
Gently mix the fresh fruit together with the rum and refrigerate. Meanwhile, bring the milk, sugar, and chocolate chips to a boil over medium heat, stirring constantly. Remove from heat, and stir in the butter and the rum. Remove the fresh fruit from the refrigerator when ready to serve and drizzle with the chocolate sauce.

 COCONUT CREME BRULEE

Ingredients:
1 cup heavy cream
1 cup fresh coconut milk
8 egg yolks
1 cup sugar
1 teaspoon vanilla extract
2 tablespoons
Callwood rum
3 tablespoons toasted flaked coconut

Locals Do It Like This:
Preheat oven to three hundred degrees. Next, combine the eggs yolks, cream, fresh coconut milk, one-third cup of sugar, vanilla, and local Callwood rum. Whisk all ingredients until silky smooth. Divide your tasty mixture between six ramekins. Place in a water bath for approximately forty-five minutes. Remove from oven and let cool before removing the ramekin dishes from the water bath. Chill for a minimum of two hours. When ready to enjoy, use two teaspoons of sugar to coat each ramekin dish. Put the finishing touches on this treat by caramelizing the custard with a butane kitchen torch until the top forms into a hard shell-like crust. Top off this dessert with toasted coconut.

CARAMELIZED BANANAS IN RUM SAUCE

Ingredients:
2 bananas
1 tbsp butter
½ vanilla pod
2 tbsp
2 tbsp superfine sugar or caster sugar
½ glass of pineapple juice
2 tbsp dark rum
1 tbsp raisins

Locals Do It Like This:
Begin by cutting the bananas in half and browning them in a frying pan with butter. Pour the sugar in to let it caramelize slowly. Add the vanilla, pineapple juice, rum, and raisins. Cover and cook for an additional 5 minutes. Coat the bananas with the sauce and serve warm.

GUAVA CAKE

Ingredients:
1 cup guava pulp
½ cup guava nectar
2 cups white sugar
1 cup butter
4 eggs
3 cups cake flour
½ teaspoon ground nutmeg
1 ¼ teaspoons baking soda
¼ teaspoon ground cloves
½ teaspoon ground cinnamon

Locals Do It Like This:
Preheat oven to 350 degrees. Sift together the nutmeg, cinnamon, cloves, flour, and baking soda. Next, combine the guava juice and guava pulp in a separate bowl. In another bowl, mix the sugar, butter, and eggs, then add the bowls of guava and flour mixtures. Pour your tasty island batter into a greased pan. Bake at 350 degrees for thirty minutes.

COOKING WITH RUM

Today, rum enjoys close to ten percent of the overall liquor market, representing not only the base for tropical cocktails but an incredibly popular flavor for many desserts. As a potent libation, rum has a minimum proof of sixty (thirty percent alcohol by volume), with plenty of stronger varieties up to 190 proof. A hot trade commodity in the Caribbean since the 1600s, rum has emerged as a cooking ingredient that is not to be underestimated:

- For a more robust flavor in your recipe, opt for a dark rum. If you're looking for a subtle taste, pick a light rum.
- Jamaican rum is often considered the strongest in flavor; its longer fermentation process utilizes previously-used yeast.
- If needed, rum extract may be substituted for small amounts of rum (no more than ¼ cup) in many recipes.
- Brandy or cognac may often be substituted for rum in equal amounts, but expect the obvious change in flavor.
- Alcohol can cause many foods to release flavors that cannot be experienced without the alcohol interaction.

Chapter Six

Island Tidbits

Looking for More Info?
Then check out the BVI Tourist Board:

Tortola
BVI Tourist Board
DeCastro Street
2nd Floor, AKARA Building
Road Town, Tortola
Tel: 284-494-3134
Fax: 284-494-3866
E-mail: info@bvitourism.com

Virgin Gorda
Virgin Gorda Yacht Harbour
Tel: 284-495-5181
Fax: 284-495-6517

Hospitals
In an emergency, Peebles Hospital is your best bet. They have surgical, x-ray and laboratory facilities. (284-494-4549/284-494-3125).

Vaccinations:
An International Vaccination Certificate is not mandatory in The British Virgin Islands.

Cruising Permits:
A permit is required for all cruising in the BVI's!

Seasonal (December 1-April 30)—All recorded Charter Boats cost $2.00 per person per day. All non-recorded Charter Boats cost $4.00 per person per day.

Out of season rates (May 1—November 30)—All recorded Charter Boats cost $0.75 per person per day. All non-recorded Charter Boats cost $4.00 per person per day.

When In Doubt, Contact the Customs Department:
It's advised that all day charter and sport fishing boats contact the British Virgin Islands Customs Department (284-494-3475 or 284-468-3701 ext. 2533) for current cruising permit requirements.

Money:
The currency of the British Virgin Islands is the U.S. dollar. In fact, the British Virgin Islands has used the dollar as its currency since 1959. Major credit cards are accepted in many, but not all, establishments. There is, however, a 10¢ stamp duty on all checks and traveler checks.

Official Language:
English

Ethnic Groups:
Black (90%), White, Chinese, Portuguese, Indian, Middle Eastern.

Religions:
Protestant 86% (Methodist 33%, Anglican 17%, Church of God 9%, Seventh-Day Adventist 5%, Baptist 4%, Jehovah's Witnesses 2%, other 2%), Roman Catholic 10%, other religion 2%, and no religion 2%.

Driving in Paradise:
The old fee of $10.00 for a temporary British Virgin Islands' Driving License has changed, folks. No longer does one need to obtain a license from the Traffic Licensing Office or from car rental agencies. Now visitors who have a valid driver's license from their home country may burn up the roads (just stay left) for up to 30 days in the BVI.

Fishing Permits:
Here's a simple rule of thumb: do not remove anything from the ocean, it's illegal. In other words, if you're a non-BVIslander without a recreational fishing permit, then leave it alone. Contact The Ministry of Natural Resources & Labour (284-468-3701 ext. 2147) for more information.

How Long Can I Stay?
Visitors may be granted entry for up to one month at the ports of entry, provided that they possess return (or ongoing) tickets, evidence of adequate means of support and pre-arranged accommodations during their stay.

But What If I Want To Stay Longer?
If you wish to extend your stay, you have to apply for an extension from the Immigration Department in Road Town, Tortola or at the Government Administration Building in Virgin Gorda. Purchase of a property in the BVI's does not, in itself, establish resident status. You can get your hands on an ID card if you're a "NonBelonger's Land Holder." Such a license allows the holder to be granted leave to stay in the BVI's for a period of up to six months in any year. However, a "Certificate of Residence," entitles the holder to remain in the BVI's for an indefinite period. You'll want to check with the Immigration Department for information regarding residency.

Do I Need a Passport?
You bet, a passport is the principal requirement for entry into the British Virgin Islands. However, Canadian and U.S. citizens may also use a birth or citizenship certificate. Visitors from some countries may require a visa for entry.

When In Doubt:
Contact the nearest BVI Tourist Board Office, the nearest British Embassy, or contact the Chief Immigration Officer at the Immigration Department of the BVI Government (284-494-3471 or 284-468-3701 ext. 2538).

Can I Use National Parks Trust Moorings?
Nope, without a permit, it's illegal. Call the National Parks Trust Office (284-494-3904) for more information.

What If I Want to Get Hitched?
Give the Registrar's Office a ring to find out about requirements: Registrar's Office, P.O. Box 418, Road Town, Tortola, British Virgin Islands or phone (284) 468-3701 or (284) 494-3492. The Registrar General can perform a civil marriage at the Registrar's Office for just $35. Or you can pick your wedding destination for a slightly higher $100 fee. A certified copy of the entry of marriage can be obtained from the Registry, for $2. E-mail: agc@mail.bvigovernment.org Web site: www.bvigovernment.org

Can I Bring Fido?
Pets are allowed entry into BVI, but only after an import permit is issued by the Department of Agriculture. For regulations governing animal importation, contact the Department of Agriculture, Paraquita Bay, Tortola, British Virgin Islands (284-495-2532 or fax to 284-495-1269).

Is There a Sales Tax?
Heck no, but there is a departure tax of $20.00 per person leaving by air, and five bucks leaving by sea and seven for cruise ship passengers.

How About a Hotel Tax?
Yes, there is a 7% Hotel Accommodation Tax payable by guests who stay for six months or less in hotels, cottages, and similar accommodations.

Where Are All the Darn ATM Machines?
If you're on Tortola check for the following (on Virgin Gorda look around at Yacht Harbour near the Bath & Turtle):

Road Town
Banco Popular
Barclays Bank
Barclays Bank at the Moorings
Chase Manhattan Bank
Barclays ATM at Pusser's Landing
H.L. Stoutt Community College, Paraquita Bay
Barclays Bank, Triple A Complex
Frenchmen's Cay
Nanny Cay
Cane Garden Bay

Major Airport:
Beef Island Airport is your best bet. There are no airports in the BVI's that are large enough for large jets. International flights are routed through St. Thomas, San Juan, or St. Martin.

Seasons:
December to May is the peak season, but the smart money is on a visit falling outside of this period. Room rates drop to around two-thirds of the rates during the busy months, and the weather calms. Between April and August is the best, and the water is the clearest. Going during the BVI Summer Fest, a two week celebration full of calypso and fungi, is always a great time!

The British Virgin Islands are the dividing line between the Atlantic Ocean, on the northern side, and the Caribbean Sea on the southern. What does that mean for you? Well, if you're a tourist you're going to be treated to a much more stable weather pattern!

BVI Population:
Approximately 22,016. Interestingly, during the last decade, the population increased some 61% with more than 80% of this increase being classified as migration.

What About the Government:
The top brass, due to the BVI's colonial relationship with the United Kingdom, is legally a constitutional democracy with the Executive Authority vested in Her Majesty, Queen Elizabeth. The Parliament or Legislative Council has thirteen representatives that are elected for a maximum of four years. The government has three branches: the Executive Council, the Judiciary, and the Legislative Council. There are over forty-five governmental departments (not including banking, electricity, and port and marine services) which are public enterprises and are owned by the Government of the British Virgin Islands. Web site: http://www.bvi.gov.vg

Capital:
Road Town, Tortola

Economy:
The BVI economy is one of the most stable and prosperous in all of the Caribbean. Highly dependent on tourism, BVI generates approximately 45% of the national income from its booming travel industry. With over 350,000 tourists (mainly from the US) flocking in every year, the 80's saw BVI offering offshore registration to companies wishing to incorporate in the islands. The BVI boasts over 450,000 companies on their offshore registry and each pays the incorporation fees to generate additional revenue for the BVI economy.

Public Holidays:
1 January—New Year's Day
Early March—H. Lavity Stoutt's Birthday (first Monday in March)
Early March—Commonwealth Day
Late March or April—Good Friday
Late March or April—Easter
30 April—Queen's Birthday
Late May or early June—Whit Monday
June—Sovereign's Birthday
1 July—Territory Day
August Monday—Starting the first Monday in August
21 October—St. Ursula's Day
25 December—Christmas Day
26 December—Boxing Day

Lay of the Land:
These are volcanic islands, so expect things to get steep and hilly in places, and flat in others. The coastal zone consists of a striking combination of beaches, mangroves, cliffs, coral reefs, and seagrass beds. The total length of beaches in the BVI is forty-nine miles. There are approximately sixty islands and cays, and only about sixteen of them are inhabited! The four major islands are Tortola, Anegada, Virgin Gorda and Jost Van Dyke.

Tides:
Each day the BVI has two high tides and two low tides, with a tidal range of a foot (30cm) to eighteen inches (45cm). The height of the tide partly depends on the atmospheric pressure.

Does Time Really Matter?
If it does, then use Atlantic Standard Time Zone year round. Remember there is no daylight saving time.

What about Cabbies?
Taxis rule if you take infrequent adventures, but a rental car (a big truck with a funky cabana style roof is always fun) is a good bet and well worth the money, especially if you like to explore the back roads and hidden beaches.

What about the Ferry?
Exploring other islands is as easy as cassava pie. Ferry rides, including trips to the U.S. Virgin Islands are frequent and abundant. Expect to pay around $20 per person, each way.

Catching the Big One:
Find yourself a pleasure fishing license or temporary fishing permit before you bait up. A pleasure fishing license is good for day sailors and recreational charter boats where guests generally use hand lines. Expect to pay $25 for a license that's good for one year. If you're a visitor that hopes to fish on charter boats and otherwise, pick up a 10-day temporary permit for $10 so you're on the up and up.

A Temporary Fishing Permit can be obtained from the Department of Conservation and Fisheries, while Commercial, Pleasure, and Sport Licenses can be obtained from the Department of Natural Resources and Labour:

Department of Conservation and Fisheries
The Quastisky Building
P.O. Box 3323
Road Town, Tortola. (284-494-5681 or 284-468-3701)
E-mail: cfd@bvigovernment.org

The Department of Natural Resources and Labour
First Floor, East Wing
Central Administration Complex
Road Town, Tortola
British Virgin Islands. (284-468-3701)
E-mail: psnrl@bvigovernment.org

Temps:
Balmy and sub-tropical, the BVI never gets too hot due to its trade winds. Rarely dropping below 77ºF (25ºC) in the winter, or rising above 90ºF (32ºC) in the summer, this island paradise averages around 83ºF (28ºC), with only slight variations between seasons. To check out daily temps, try the following reliable sites operated by BVIslanders:
www.DearMissMermaid.com
www.WeatherBVI.com
www.StormCarib.com

Digits:
If you're ringing in from North America, make sure to dial 1 + 284 + the seven-digit local number. Everyone else—dial your country's direct dialing prefix + 1 + 284 + the seven-digit local number.

Duds:
Things are pretty casual but don't go showing off your bare assets around town. Low-key is fine, just keep the skinny-dipping and streaking on the down low so as not to offend.

What Should I Expect To Pay?

Expect to fork over at least US$200 a day for comfortable lodging on land and at a minimum US$250 on a chartered yacht. You may be able to squeak out a trip on less by traveling during the low season, researching guest houses, and seeking out campgrounds.

Capture It:

Don't opt for just any photographer; seek out Jim Scheiner (284-494-2749) to book custom videos, underwater portraits, camera rentals, and film processing.

Whale Watchin':

Look for humpback whales, along with their calves, from January to mid-March. You'll spot mother whales swimming at the surface with their calves. Look for an exhalation spout (along with a deep hiss) anywhere from the ocean north of Virgin Gorda to The Dogs. Other good places for whale watching include Copper Mine Point on Virgin Gorda, Carrot Bay, and just outside of South Sound.

Looking for Sea Turtles:

Look carefully around turtle grass, the endangered green sea turtle's favorite treat. You'll also find sea turtles nesting on Tortola's Lambert Bay and Anegada's ocean coast beaches.

Great Snorkel Locations: Check out the seagrass beds and sea turtles at Trellis Bay, The Bight at Norman Island, North Sound, Deadman's Bay, Manchioneel Bay at Cooper Island, White Bay on Peter Island, and The Baths and Little Trunk Bay on Virgin Gorda.

The Best Waves:

Apple Bay on Tortola is always a crowd pleaser. Try hitting the waves when the wind is coming from the southeast. Best of all, if the waves aren't happenin' then you always have nearby Bomba Shack as a solid back-up for seaside entertainment.

Searching for Tarpon:

Look for this large silvery fish at White Bay on Jost Van Dyke and around Saba Rock.

How About Something Different on Anegada?

Check out the Iguana Repopulation project, featuring a breeding ground for iguanas and juveniles waiting to be released. The perfect treat for feral cats, native iguanas are getting a little boost from islanders. Stop by the police station and poke around the side yard to take a look.

Webcams:

www.sabarock.com
www.nannycay.com/webcam.htm
www.leverickbay.org/webcam.htm
www.cooperisland-bvi.com/QAN_Webcam1.htm
www.reservationsbvi.com/web%20cams/heritage%20inn.html
www.reservationsbvi.com/cam/pusserrt.html
www.reservationsbvi.com/cam/roadharbour.html

Best Way to Get Around:

Tortola is among the friendliest of the islands, and catching a cab or ride with the locals is easy enough. Plus, biking and walking are good ways to get a feel for the land, especially if you're close to the port in Road Town. Keep in mind, though, the land is hilly, making walking or biking difficult if you'd like to see all the sights. Many folks opt to rent a car for a few days just to feel good about seeing all of the island. A few suggestions for quality rental agencies are as follows:

Speedy's Car Rental: P.O. Box 35, The Valley, Virgin Gorda, BVI
Tel.: (284) 495-5240, 495-5235, 495-5779 Fax: (284) 495-5755 VHF Ch. 16
E-mail: speedysbvi@surfbvi.com

Dollar Rent A Car
Prospect Reef and Long Bay Beach Resort Address:
P.O. Box 3305, Road Town, Tortola, BVI
(284-494-6093 fax to 284-494-7837)
E-mail: dollar@caribsurf.com
Facilities: Renting Suzuki Side Kicks—featuring four-wheel drive, AC or soft-top.
Rates: Summer: $40—$65 per day; Winter: $55—$65 per day. Available at both locations.

Hertz Car Rental West End Address:
P.O.Box 1060, West End, Tortola, BVI
(International: 800-654-3080 or 284-495-4405. fax to 284-494-6060)
E-mail: hertzbvi@hotmail.com

Send-A-Chef-To-School

A portion of the sales of *British Virgin Islands: The Hometown Lowdown Guide to Travel and Taste* will be awarded to a budding local BVI chef to attend culinary class. If you'd like to recommend your favorite chef-in-the-making, please visit www.islandlowdown.com to nominate your favorite kitchen phenom. All nominees should demonstrate a reliance on local ingredients, produce, and appreciation of BVI recipes.

About the Author

Paul Spicer, an award-winning author and columnist, is known for lively tales of off-beat travel along with colorful characters and nightlife from the international stage. From food and spirits to art and entertainment, his work has graced the covers of worldwide publications. He has served as a travel writer for North Star Travel Media, Weissmann Travel Reports, and International Living, while his food and drink reviews regularly appear in Brick Weekly, Patterson's Beverage Review, and Karma Magazine. Spicer has also created his own ice cream flavor, Cappuccino Crème Brule with Shortbread Cookies, for Bev's Ice Cream, with all proceeds directed towards a non profit organization. Continuing to publish works related to fun, food, and travel—a portion of the sales of British Virgin Islands: The Hometown Lowdown Guide to Travel & Taste will help support new chefs with an interest in local ingredients and BVI recipes. With tucked away island destinations serving as his subject matter, Spicer has created Island Lowdown Press, along with online communities at www.igoiwrite.com and www.islandlowdown.com, for adventure seekers to share their travel secrets and converse with local chefs, business owners, hotel owners, and fellow travelers.

Index